Are Evangelical Christians Hypocrites?

Are Evangelical Christians Hypocrites?

How Being Born-Again Transforms People and Shapes Their Worldview

DAVID CULVER BRENNER

WIPF & STOCK · Eugene, Oregon

ARE EVANGELICAL CHRISTIANS HYPOCRITES?
How Being Born-Again Transforms People and Shapes Their Worldview

Copyright © 2025 David Culver Brenner. All rights reserved. Except for brief quotations in critical publications or reviews, no part of this book may be reproduced in any manner without prior written permission from the publisher. Write: Permissions, Wipf and Stock Publishers, 199 W. 8th Ave., Suite 3, Eugene, OR 97401.

Wipf & Stock
An Imprint of Wipf and Stock Publishers
199 W. 8th Ave., Suite 3
Eugene, OR 97401

www.wipfandstock.com

PAPERBACK ISBN: 979-8-3852-3051-8
HARDCOVER ISBN: 979-8-3852-3052-5
EBOOK ISBN: 979-8-3852-3053-2
VERSION NUMBER 07/30/25

Scriptures taken from the Holy Bible, New International Version®, NIV®. Copyright © 1973, 1978, 1984, 2011 by Biblica, Inc.™ Used by permission of Zondervan. All rights reserved worldwide, www.zondervan.com. The "NIV" and "New International Version" are trademarks registered in the United States Patent and Trademark Office by Biblica, Inc.™

This book is dedicated to my amazing wife, Kristen, with much love and gratitude for her encouragement, long-suffering, and faithfulness during the writing of this book.

Contents

Preface | ix
Acknowledgments | xii

PART ONE: What Evangelicals Believe

A   Are Evangelical Christians Hypocrites?
1   What Evangelicals Believe Versus How They Behave | 5
2   How Can Evangelicals Possibly Think They're Right with God Apart from How They Actually Behave? | 10
3   What Evangelicals Believe About Themselves Is Terrifying! | 13
4   Spiritual Babies | 17
5   Works Without Faith | 21
6   Why Only Christians Can Please God | 25
7   Restricted to Sinners Only | 29
8   Evangelical Christianity's Big Flaws | 33
9   Evangelical Christianity Is Only for Straight, White People, Right? | 36
10 How Being an Evangelical Christian Is Harder than Being an Unbeliever | 40
11 Why You (Probably) Don't Need to Fear Genuine Evangelical Believers | 44
12 When Evangelical Christians Don't Act Like It | 46
13 Why Are There So Many Fake Christians? | 50
14 How Can You Tell If Someone's Truly Saved? | 55

- B Don't Bite the Book That Feeds You | 59
- C The Upside-Down Kingdom | 77

PART TWO: How Evangelical Christians See the World
- A Kindly Stop Stealing from My Worldview | 83
- B The Imaginary World of John Lennon | 89
- C Why Evangelicals Oppose Multiculturalism | 99
- D The Biblical Worldview, Sphere Sovereignty, and Evangelicalism's Complicated Relationship with the State | 105

Bibliography | 111

Preface

OVER THE LAST DECADE, much has been said and written concerning the political activity of "born-again" Christians. Widespread support from Evangelicals for President Donald Trump has surely raised concerns among non-Evangelicals on how born-again religiosity influences political beliefs and activity. Yet, politics is in fact only a small part of the overall experience and focus of Protestant evangelical believers ("Evangelicals") who live under a mandate to seek and know God in order that they might live in conformity with his purposes. It is likely, then, that the outsized attention on evangelical politics has skewed and truncated the public understanding of what it means to be born again and why and how evangelical faith transforms believers beyond politics and impacts how they see the world.

I seek in this book to address misimpressions of Evangelicalism and bring clarity to what Evangelicals believe, how evangelical faith plays out practically in the lives of believers, and how it shapes the worldview of Evangelicals, including their sense of what social and political arrangements serve humanity best. In order to accomplish this, I've taken several different approaches, which include discussing key theological doctrines and their impact on believers; contrasting Evangelicalism with worldviews that largely contradict it, such as materialism and multiculturalism; and engaging critics and skeptics of the Bible's validity and relevance today.

Preface

In the first section of this book, I seek to explain Evangelicalism by focusing mostly on four essentials that loom large in the lives of Evangelicals: (1) the absolute reliability of Scripture in the original texts, or "inerrancy"; (2) being "born again," or the miracle of conversion, as the indispensable initiating work of salvation; (3) grace, or salvation as a gift rather than as a reward for good works; and (4) faith in Christ alone as the only means of becoming right with God, also known as "justification," a corollary of which is that no one can be made right with God by some combination—say, fifty-fifty or seventy-thirty—of faith and works. Faith in the justifying work of Christ is the necessary and exclusively sufficient means of salvation for Evangelicals.

It should be noted that Evangelicals disagree on whether faith precedes (the Arminian view) or comes after (the Calvinistic view) conversion (or "regeneration"). But the means by which all Evangelicals are made right with God is the same: faith alone. As the differences between Arminians and Calvinists largely do not pertain to the discussion herein, there was no need to distinguish between the two camps. Arminians and Calvinists often worship together in the same churches, and within Evangelicalism, neither view is deemed to be at odds with Christian orthodoxy.

Yet, I want to be clear that this is not a book of theology, and while the above beliefs are, in my view, the most pertinent to understanding how Evangelicals live out their faith in the real world, they are not anywhere close to being exhaustive of evangelical theology.

Also, while these four theological ideas are central to Evangelicalism, they also are either countercultural or counterintuitive; consequently, they are often misunderstood, even among Evangelicals. For instance, a national survey of two thousand Americans in 2020 by Arizona Christian University found that 41 percent of the survey participants attending evangelical churches said they "believe that a person can qualify for Heaven by being or doing good."[1] This book, therefore, is as much for Evangelicals themselves as it is for those who are not.

---

1. Klett, "Half of US Christians."

Preface

The second section of the book reflects on the worldview that typically flows from Evangelicalism, principally by comparing Evangelicalism to competing worldviews. As regards Evangelicals' participation in America's public debate and politics, I am persuaded that Evangelicals' voting tracks more closely with biblically formed concerns, rather than with the charisma and communication styles of leading voices in these realms. Accordingly, my treatment of public issues looks upstream to see how fidelity to evangelical scriptural imperatives, and the "good and necessary consequences" of evangelical biblical theology, inform born-again believers' views on the proper role of government and other God-ordained institutions.

Given that the sole focus of this book is on evangelical beliefs and practices, no one should draw any conclusions regarding the other branches of Christianity, or about other strains of Protestantism, from it. Of course, there will be significant overlap with Christian churches and denominations outside of Evangelicalism. Nonetheless, the absence of any discussion of other Christian denominations should not be interpreted as implicit commentary, positive or negative, regarding other forms of Christian belief, practice, and expression. I am an Evangelical, and my principal religious interest and expertise concerns Evangelicalism—hence, the book's subject.

Finally, readers will no doubt take notice of my inherent bias on the subject matter and naturally will assess the approach and content accordingly. While I have sought to convey evangelical beliefs as fairly and sensitively as possible for non-evangelical readers, my point of view and preferences are not hard to discern. This book, then, is an "insider's" account and therefore necessarily partisan. Nonetheless, hopefully it sheds some light on how Evangelicals see themselves and how they seek to understand and engage the world around them—or, at a bare minimum, how one Evangelical does.

David Culver Brenner

Acknowledgments

THANKS SO MUCH TO Ann Plank and Dorothy Moore for reading an early draft and providing very helpful feedback and suggestions.

I am also very grateful for the prayers, support, and encouragement of Samuel Nageli and Vinaya Prakasham, as well as that of the Leesburg Community Group at Hamilton Baptist Church.

Thanks also to Pancho, our "Staffy" mix, who stayed close to my side while I worked on this book.

Part One

What Evangelicals Believe

A

Are Evangelical Christians Hypocrites?

1

What Evangelicals Believe Versus How They Behave

INTRODUCTION

PEOPLE OUTSIDE OF EVANGELICAL Christian belief likely notice discrepancies between the behavior of Evangelicals and Christian preaching about right and wrong. It's quite natural that such observations should arise—it touches upon what is undeniably true. If they are honest, Evangelicals must admit to them.

We know of an unbeliever who was upset that an evangelical mom she knows didn't want her fifteen-year-old son to have a friendship with a non-Christian girl he'd been spending time with. The person sharing this said it was unchristian of the mom to bar her son's friendship with an unbeliever. For all we know, the evangelical mom was fully justified in her concern about her son's relationship with this girl, particularly in the light of surging teen hormones. But, for the sake of argument, let's just say the unbeliever's assessment of the mom as behaving "unchristian" was correct. What should we conclude when Evangelicals fail to live up to their billing?

A: Are Evangelical Christians Hypocrites?

A COMMON MISUNDERSTANDING OF WHAT MAKES ONE AN EVANGELICAL CHRISTIAN

Christianity addresses the problem of God's moral perfection and our radical imperfection. As unbelievers move toward faith, their awareness of the vast chasm between God and themselves deepens. Their desperate need for a way to traverse that impossible distance is revealed to them by grace, or God's unmerited favor. They become believers because God makes their need of a merciful go-between—that is, Christ—known to them. Evangelicals believe he is the only one who can bridge that chasm on their behalf. They are broken sinners who find mercy and begin on the path of restoration and newness of life. This is the starting point of a lifetime journey of faith and repentance.

It's not hard for those outside Evangelical Protestant faith to see the inevitable contradictions between how Evangelicals live and the righteousness that God demands. And so, the charge of hypocrisy is often leveled: "You believe you should live this way, but you do not," unbelievers may think, or even say out loud. This reaction is understandable, despite being deeply mistaken.

It would be hypocritical if Evangelicals claimed to be perfectly righteous. The very fact they are not is what brings them to Christ. They agree that his perfectly righteous laws are right, and their way of living is wrong. But, as is often the case in twenty-first-century American culture, merely professing a belief in moral truth is enough to elicit charges of being judgmental, self-righteous, and hypocritical.

That response typically is a defense mechanism. Folks naturally feel threatened when anyone holds to absolute moral standards—and what it implies for themselves. Few welcome the news that they are accountable to a perfectly holy God. Hence, the reactionary and incoherent response to Evangelicals carrying the gospel is sometimes "Hypocrite!"—thus reassuring unbelievers that since Evangelicals don't keep their own moral precepts, no one else is required to, either.

A valid—but not necessarily recommended—response to such an accusation might be: "I envy you. No one can ever accuse you of being a hypocrite since you don't subscribe to any unbending moral standards. It must be nice to have a pliable morality that accommodates new circumstances."

Of course, when someone who rejects moral truth is lied to, stolen from, or cheated on, all of a sudden those fixed moral laws seem fairly self-evident, and even quite practical.

Okay, so now we know, as the bumper sticker says, "Christians aren't perfect, just forgiven." But then what is expected of believers, aside from plastering a cheesy bumper sticker on the back of the minivan?

WHAT IS REQUIRED OF EVANGELICAL CHRISTIANS?

We've noticed that Christian Evangelicals don't claim to be perfect—indeed, their admitted sinfulness is what draws them to Christ. So, if they don't or can't obey God's laws, what is expected of them?

Make no mistake, Jesus commands moral perfection. He says, "Be perfect, therefore, as your heavenly Father is perfect" (Matt 5:48), but certainly not as a condition of salvation. If attaining perfection is what defined a Christian, there would be no such thing as a Christian.

When asked directly what was required to inherit eternal life, Jesus simply answered, "To believe in the one he has sent" (John 6:29)—in other words, to believe in Jesus. That's it, the sum total of his answer! This astonishing claim is difficult for us to fathom and accept. "There must be something else—or else a lot of really bad folks will be getting into heaven," we instinctively reason—especially when we assume the bad folks don't include us.

In short, God's incredible gift of forgiveness to sinners is hard for anyone—Christian and non-Christian alike—to wrap their heads around. Christians will spend a lifetime marveling at God's mercy. It's not at all surprising that skeptics would scoff at what Christians claim to be the gift of God's unmerited favor (grace).

A: Are Evangelical Christians Hypocrites?

Why should Christians, or anyone for that matter, get off scot-free merely by believing that over two millennia ago some guy on a cross made everything right?

Surely, the skeptics have a point: that God pardons, and even exalts and eternally blesses the vilest of sinners, seems too good to be true. But its very incomprehensibility argues against it being a human invention. In all other religions, attaining the object of one's faith—heaven, nirvana, etc.—requires great personal moral effort. That is a far different bargain from the salvation offered by Christianity, which declares, "For the wages of sin is death, but the gift of God is eternal life in Christ Jesus our Lord" (Rom 6:23). When anyone in a TV ad says, "And get this free gift," our antennae naturally go up. There's nothing that's truly free (certainly not lunch), we assume.

In short, the only qualification to become an Evangelical is being a sinner. Certainly not you, dear reader! But the rest of us are amply and even overqualified.

Hence, the free offer of peace with God and eternal blessedness raises a troubling question: How can people sorely lacking in virtue be accepted by a holy God? God's unmerited favor, or grace, challenges expectations and even offends our sense of justice. Who'd guess that God forgives and receives as beloved children those who formerly were thieves, murderers, liars, adulterers, fornicators, blasphemers, and so on (1 Cor 6:9–11)?

It's a paradox that God calls and redeems many of the worst of us. So, the very idea of grace lends itself to the charge of hypocrisy.

Evangelicals claim that God's love has been peculiarly lavished upon them, such that their worst sins are forever erased, as well as future sins. That belief seems like a recipe for a sense of moral superiority and a lack of empathy for those who aren't "right" with God, not to mention an ugly pridefulness.

One might rightly wonder how these evangelical Christians—who are convinced they're right with God despite few or any good deeds to show—will behave. Isn't that like spoiling a child who inevitably turns into an insufferable monster?

What Evangelicals Believe Versus How They Behave

But perhaps there are credible reasons to believe that these believers are accepted and loved by God, even though they are greatly undeserving of it. It's certainly counterintuitive because that's not how we humans typically roll—we're big on expecting folks to do right by us as a condition of our acceptance and love. So, understanding why Evangelicals think they're okay with God may be the key to figuring out whether or not they're hypocrites, or possibly just insane.

2

How Can Evangelicals Possibly Think They're Right with God Apart from How They Actually Behave?

SKEPTICS MAY VIEW THE evangelical Christian belief that salvation is an unearned gift from God disconcerting. There's nothing scarier than people who think God loves and favors them for no other reason than they're convinced it's true, or because some primitive holy book says so, the arguments go.

How Evangelicals can possibly believe such a thing, at first blush, will certainly not reassure the wary. Many have heard that on the cross Christ, who is God incarnate (or "God in the flesh"), paid for the sins of those who trust him for salvation. It's astounding and seemingly far-fetched that a holy God would become a man in order to suffer and die in the place of chronic lawbreakers.

The Evangelical believes that Christ's death satisfied God's justice—or, more simply, the need to punish our sins. Scripture asserts, "For Christ also suffered once for sins, the righteous for the unrighteous, to bring you to God" (1 Pet 3:18a). The morally perfect One suffered and died for the multitude of morally sick ones. So, God doesn't overlook the sins of believers but instead accounted for them fully through Jesus' death. As many have observed, God's love for sinful men and women and his hatred of sin met at the cross. But this is only the half of it.

The Evangelical idea of grace is something even grander, which the unbelieving skeptic may see as even more worrisome than the mere canceling of the penalty for sins.

Scripture not only says the sins of believers no longer count against them but that Christ's perfect record of obedience on earth is transferred and applied to them also. The apostle Paul writes, "For as by the one man's disobedience [Adam] the many were made sinners, so by the one man's obedience [Jesus] the many will be made righteous" (Rom 5:19).

Evangelical Christians thus possess a vicarious righteousness that is, well, perfect. And it is a fundamental aspect of Christian salvation because, as Micah McCormick explains,

> Christ's obedience brings [believers] . . . to a status beyond being simply forgiven. As stunning as it is to believe that we no longer face God's eternal punishment, often Christians still labor under a sense of guilt, knowing that we are not the kind of people that we should be. But God has not only removed our filthy clothes, he has given us clean clothes (Zech. 3:4–5). We are not merely pardoned criminals. We are also beloved sons and daughters with whom God is well pleased, because we are united to Christ our head, and our obedience remains at God's right hand, completely unassailable.[1]

By virtue of Christ's righteousness attributed to followers, Christians are vastly holier than unbelievers, which is why the New Testament audaciously refers to believers as "saints." Again, while not an inherent righteousness, in God's sight believers are credited with the exact same righteousness achieved on earth as Christ himself (2 Cor 5:21, Rom 5:19).

The writers of the New Testament are able to call fellow believers "saints" because their new status as God's adopted children,

---

1. McCormick, "Obedience and Sinlessness."

A: Are Evangelical Christians Hypocrites?

clothed in the righteousness of Christ, is an immediate, present, and irrevocable reality. So certain and unchangeable is this reality upon conversion that Paul tells fellow believers, "God raised us up with Christ and seated us with him in the heavenly realms in Christ Jesus" (Eph 2:6). Paul is using the past tense here, thereby telling converts that their adoption into God's family and possession of eternal life is unequivocally and forever a done deal.

Those familiar with the Old Testament may recognize this idea of imputed righteousness through faith. In the book of Genesis, Abraham was gifted a righteousness he didn't possess and hadn't earned. Scripture says, "Abraham believed God, and it was credited to him as righteousness" (Gen 15:6). So, the idea of God conferring righteousness on someone merely on the basis of belief actually appears in the very first book of the Bible.

The practical benefit of the new legal status given to the Christian—from guilty to not guilty and unrighteous to righteous—is enormous. How can sinners have assurance that God hears the prayers of—to paraphrase the prophet Isaiah—a people with unclean lips living among unclean people (Isa 6:5)? Christians have confidence God hears them because they approach him on the basis of Christ's perfect record. That permits absolute, unflinching confidence.

All of this likely is *not* reassuring to the unbeliever. It may even seem like we're trying to make the case that Christians are not only hypocrites, but dangerous lunatics! "You mean, these Jesus freaks see themselves as possessing a vastly superior righteousness than those who don't follow Jesus? Isn't that an invitation for Christians to look down on others and even mistreat them?" We'll seek to unravel this mystery next.

3

What Evangelicals Believe About Themselves Is Terrifying!

EVANGELICAL CHRISTIANS, AS NOTED, though not righteous in and of themselves, possess the vicarious or imputed righteousness of Christ through faith. Not only are the sins of believers paid for and forgiven, but Christ's own righteousness is credited to them, thus restoring a right relationship between them and God.

That could well startle and scare unbelievers. One would rightly be afraid of people who are convinced that God adores them but alternatively will cast those who deny and reject Jesus Christ, the Son of God, into the agonies of hell.

The New Testament even admits that the radical grace it proclaims is dangerous and prone to being abused. Paul, the writer of the book of Romans, exhorts believers not to misuse grace: "What shall we say then? Are we to continue in sin that grace may abound? By no means! How can we who died to sin still live in it?" (Rom 6:1–2). No doubt, it's possible that Evangelicals could assume that God's forgiveness for past, present, and future sins is a license to misbehave, but they'd have to ignore the many admonitions against sin by Paul and Jesus (John 8:12, Matt 4:17).

A: Are Evangelical Christians Hypocrites?

Nonetheless, skeptics might still ask, "If Evangelical converts are still sinners, why would anyone trust them any more than a sinful unbeliever?" This is because, for Evangelicals, while conversion is a no-strings-attached gift of grace, Evangelicalism also holds that genuine conversion is always accompanied by some sign(s) of transformation and repentance. Evangelicals are, after all, "new creations" according to Scripture (2 Cor 5:17). In short, the spiritual birth of the new believer always produces some righteous fruit, even if it's not yet as sweet as a ripe mango.

If evangelical Christianity is a delusion, and "conversion" in fact changed no one in a supernatural way, one would have to concede that Evangelicalism could be a scary invitation to a harmful sense of moral superiority.

But if, instead, conversion is a supernatural event in which a new believer is made spiritually alive, moral transformation will be real and readily observable. It will be apparent in a convert's reoriented priorities, a new hatred of and struggle against sin, and new convictions to love God and neighbor. Genuine believers are called and equipped to live as Christ did, and will start on that path—at a minimum—in small but meaningful ways. In many cases, the changes will even be quite obvious and dramatic. (The transformation of the "Son of Sam," a notorious serial killer, is one such example.[1])

That doesn't necessarily make a new evangelical Christian morally better than any particular unbeliever in daily life. It may be that an egregiously horrible person, after conversion, is better than he was previously but still far less "moral" than an upright unbeliever. We all start out from different places—we are "good" or "bad" people, relative to fallen humanity, based on the varying inputs of nature and nurture (largely beyond our control) we received. Nonetheless, a true conversion should evince "before" and "after" images that are noticeably different.

If you didn't know a particular Evangelical before they were saved, you may be surprised that such an awful person is actually redeemed. Many times, the best post-conversion testimony an

---

1. Berkowitz, "My Testimony."

Evangelical can summon is, "You should have seen me before I got saved."

Nonetheless, some positive changes in the convert's life should be observable. Evangelicals will also assure others that they are not working to earn salvation and thus are trying to obey God for an entirely different reason. We'll tackle that next.

A NEW CREATION, BUT STILL A WORK IN PROGRESS

As noted earlier, Evangelicals believe that salvation and conversion are gifts that can't be earned. Salvation by grace alone through the instrumentality of faith alone—via a supernatural work of conversion—is so central to Evangelical Christianity that if anyone asserts the counter-scriptural claim that they have earned or are earning their salvation, they clearly are not saved. They've missed the gospel entirely.

Belief systems in which salvation is achieved through effort lend themselves to the pride of accomplishment. Evangelicalism utterly precludes that. Evangelicals instead must acknowledge that they deserve condemnation and hell rather than an eternally blessed existence in God's presence. Consequently, an Evangelical is obliged to live in humility and gratitude, especially since salvation depends on an innocent man bearing the torture and death he or she should have borne.

Evangelicals are to love, serve, and obey God. The Bible—which Evangelicals believe is God's inspired and infallible message—actually says that loving and obeying Christ are virtually one and the same. "If you love me, you will keep my commandments" (John 14:15), Jesus says. And Scripture—that is, God himself, Evangelicals insist—continually commands humility and gentleness, while insisting that believers consider others as more important than themselves (Eph 4:2a, Phil 2:3b).

Nonetheless, the reason for obedience is not to win God's acceptance, forgiveness, and eternal life. Those are gifts of salvation. Rather, Evangelicals seek to imitate God out of love and gratitude, as the indwelling Holy Spirit, the third person of the Trinity (consisting of Father, Son, and Holy Spirit), now guides and helps them in their new calling. The apostle Paul explains, "For it is God who works in you to will and to act in order to fulfill his good purpose" (Phil 2:13).

However, the Evangelical's attempts to obey this calling and thus walk in holiness is far from automatic or passive. It requires the believer to intentionally submit to God and die to self, especially as Evangelicals are to love and sacrifice even for their enemies. The Evangelical's Holy Spirit–enabled life is to be characterized by "love, joy, peace, forbearance, kindness, goodness, faithfulness, and self-control" (Gal 5:22–23).

Often, an Evangelical's feelings are at odds with God's commands. It's not unusual for an Evangelical to feel intense dislike for a neighbor or coworker. Evangelicals don't have to live in denial about their feelings regarding obnoxious, hard-to-love people. But they aren't to act on those feelings. In a sense, this is when the Evangelical is allowed and even encouraged to be a hypocrite. Evangelicals are called to love others despite inwardly feeling the opposite. You might say they are called to be "phonies" by acting in loving ways to people they don't feel an iota of love toward while they pray for a genuine change of heart. But an Evangelical isn't to wait for a change of heart before acting lovingly. Believers are to obey God, not their feelings. Often, acting contrary to one's feelings is the key to a real change in feelings, as C. S. Lewis elucidates in his classic book, *Mere Christianity*.[2]

If you've seen Evangelicals who don't behave lovingly, you may be unconvinced that Christ really changes people. Evangelicals must admit they don't come close to mirroring the life that Jesus lived. Evangelical believers still succumb to sin each and every day. Why do these "born-again" Evangelicals live such schizophrenic lives? We'll need to go back in time to unpack that enigma.

---

2. Lewis, *Mere Christianity*, 63.

4

Spiritual Babies

WE STARTED THIS BOOK by observing that evangelical Christians often don't live up to their billing. They are supposed to be Christ-like—full of good deeds and love toward their neighbors. That's frequently not the case. Hence, when unbelievers see this incongruity, they may question or even dismiss the legitimacy of Christianity itself.

This conundrum requires that we back up a bit—all the way to the beginning—because unbelievers who reach such a conclusion usually do so out of a very different perspective on the cause of humanity's problems.

Evangelical Christianity posits that the fundamental crisis in all of our lives is not simply disregarding God's laws—that's merely the symptom of our inherited relational problem. We are deeply estranged from God, according to Scripture. The very first sin was not that Adam and Eve ate the forbidden fruit.[1] For Evangelicals, the first sin took place in their thinking just prior to that, wherein they doubted God's goodness and veracity. As a result,

---

1. Although many today view the story of Adam and Eve as a fable, Jesus did not: he understood it as historically real and true (Matt 19:4).

they disregarded the only prohibition God had given to them: to not eat the fruit of the tree of the knowledge of good and evil. Instead, they listened to and acted upon the serpent's lies that God wasn't being straight with, and unfairly withholding good, from them (Gen 3).

By preferring the serpent's lies—"Surely, you will certainly not die," and "You will be like God" (Gen 3:4–5)—rather than trusting God, Adam and Eve destroyed their deep intimacy with God. Yet, despite their rebellion, God extends grace to Adam and Eve by providing animal skins to cover their newly discovered nakedness, and he delays the sentence of physical death he'd warned them of. He imposes consequences for their rebellion but also announces a plan to restore their lost intimacy with him (Gen 3:15–19).

Evangelicals believe that Adam and Eve represented all of humankind; therefore, everyone is born into this broken relationship with God. (That may seem unfair, but we can logically surmise that we would have done no better.) As a result, from birth, all people naturally take it upon themselves to decide what is "good" and what is "evil." The default setting of all human hearts, Evangelicals believe, is to do whatever pleases us, without considering God's will for us. Our misery proceeds from this self-autonomy because while our conscience still alerts us to right and wrong, we foolishly ignore and suppress these "alerts" in favor of our own wants and desires. But our own ideas about what will make us happy fail time and time again, while we pile up guilt and grow ever more distant from God, posit Evangelicals.

At bottom, according to Evangelicalism, humankind doesn't trust God to know what's best for us, and we strongly prefer that our Creator, Provider, and Sustainer keep a safe distance. Humankind's rejection of and hostility toward God drives the unrelenting mayhem we see in and all around us. For Evangelicals, all human disharmony is traceable to the "sin nature" inside of us, rather than factors that are outside of us.

Accordingly, Evangelicals believe that a relationship of trust between God and individuals must be restored before any of us can do good rather than evil. That relationship is the foundation

Spiritual Babies

for all good works, which are motivated by love for and faith in God, in keeping with Scripture, say Evangelicals (Heb 11:6).

Thus, for Evangelicals that means trusting in God's goodness and righteousness and leaning on Christ alone for salvation. Good works that please God can only spring from that kind of faith and a heart intent on magnifying and glorifying God rather than oneself. It is the faith we discussed earlier, proceeding from the miracle of regeneration, or being "born again." Evangelicals insist on the necessity of being "born again," as Jesus did in the third chapter of the gospel of John.

Still, after their saving encounter with Christ, believers are just spiritual babies. Moving toward complete trust and reliance on God and his revealed will is typically a long, slow process involving many stumbles and falls. (Evangelicals can easily relate to the accounts of the Old Testament patriarchs as evidence of this rollercoaster experience.) It often takes many years of repeated failures and continual, daily repentance before evangelical believers are able to fully renounce long-standing sinful behaviors.

The fancy-pants theologians call this process of renouncing sin and embracing holiness "sanctification," and it is nourished through the ministrations of the local church through Bible teaching and study, worship, prayer, fellowship with other believers, and the sacraments. And again, unlike conversion, sanctification is hardly a passive process; rather, it requires great intentionality and perseverance on the part of the believer.

Yet, once again, the important thing to note is that all spiritual progress for the evangelical believer is an outgrowth of a renewed relationship with God through faith in Christ. God's intention for the believer is that he or she become Christ-like—he aims to fill the universe with mini-Christs, who resemble God in holiness, in part because our eternal happiness depends on it. Evangelicals say that sin brings misery in the long run and even greater misery beyond death, apart from salvation.

Evangelicals believe that the misery caused by sin is something everyone will experience to some degree, Evangelical and non-Evangelical alike, because our misdeeds boomerang back to us sooner or later. In his work *The Problem of Pain*, C. S. Lewis estimates that 80 percent of our suffering is the direct result of our own sin.[2] We'll take the "over" on that one.

It turns out that the answer to the reasonable question "Aren't evangelical Christians supposed to be loving and do good deeds?" is a resounding yes, but with the caveat that it takes new converts time to learn how to live out their faith and establish new holy habits; so this process typically starts with tentative baby steps, and it will remain unfinished until we die.

Yet, as a result of the restored relationship between God and believers, Evangelicals are now able to perform good deeds that are pleasing to God. In fact, only the good deeds of "born-again" Christians are pleasing to him. We'll unpack that "punch in the nose" assertion shortly.

---

2. Lewis, *Problem of Pain*, 89.

5

Works Without Faith

WE ENDED THE LAST chapter by saying only Christians can do good deeds that are pleasing to God. No, we really aren't trying to deliberately make you angry or run for the blood pressure medicine. So before you throw a kitchen appliance at us, allow us to explain why Evangelicals hold to this controversial idea. Not surprisingly, many folks, even some Evangelicals, struggle with it.

First, the Bible portrays God as infinitely loving but also as infinitely holy and just. Perhaps when we discussed the broken relationship between God and humankind, it seemed drastic and cruel that God required the torture and murder of his Son in order to restore that relationship. After all, all Adam and Eve did was to eat some forbidden fruit. But it's hard for us, as fallen creatures, to envisage the depth of betrayal and degeneracy in this act, given God's holy character.

Adam and Eve were made by God and declared by him to be "very good" (Gen 1:31). There wasn't the tiniest speck of darkness in them—their hearts and minds were absolutely pure. As such, they enjoyed perfect communion with God in the garden—with no sin to obscure their relationship with him or each other. They enjoyed this loving fellowship in the paradise God created for them, and he sustained them moment by moment both physically and spiritually.

Moreover, he'd only restricted them from eating the fruit from one tree—they could eat any other of the delicacies in this garden. In short, God is saying, "I am the Creator and you are my beloved creatures—don't break our fellowship by coveting and trying to usurp my role as lawgiver and King." When they violated this command, they didn't just get caught with their hands in the cookie jar. They presumed the right to define good and evil—to become like God—thus trampling upon and usurping the sole prerogative of their Creator, as Satan himself had done. They jettisoned their creaturely role in a failed coup to replace the King on the throne. It was truly an act of treachery.

THE UNIVERSAL FRUIT OF REBELLION

Having failed to honor the one simple command, they reaped the promised fruit of their rebellion: death. By grace, God delayed their physical death but not their spiritual death. We see this in their attempt to hide from God after sinning and, perhaps most conspicuously, in how Adam responds when God asks him if he'd eaten the fruit: "The man [Adam] said, 'The woman you put here with me—she gave me some fruit from the tree, and I ate it'" (Gen 3:12).

Even though he'd been right at Eve's side when she took the fruit and offered it to him, Adam lays the blame at her feet. Adam's spiritual death was manifested in his quickness to deny and shift responsibility, a habit that continues to this day in every one of us.

As a result of Adam's rebellion, Evangelicals say, Scripture declares that all subsequent people have been born spiritually dead; accordingly, every single one of us is naturally opposed to the ways of God from birth and is under his wrath.

The idea of God being wrathful may seem jarring to us, but could anyone take God seriously if he was okay with the unrelenting wickedness we see all around and in us day after day (Eph

2:1–3)? Even we, as fallen creatures, can agree with the bumper sticker sentiment, "If you're not angry, you're not paying attention"—at least with regard to the sins of others, if not our own.

Evangelicals cite both the Old and New Testaments as attesting to the dire condition of spiritually dead humankind in the sight of God:

> There is no one righteous, not even one;
> there is no one who understands;
> there is no one who seeks God.
> All have turned away,
> they have together become worthless;
> there is no one who does good,
> not even one. (Rom 3:10–12)[1]

This is somewhat shocking. "Really, no one seeks God?" one may ask. "How about the seven billion or so who subscribe to belief in a deity?"

The evangelical answer is that no one by nature seeks the one true God, and no one is able to please God in his or her natural state of alienation from him. Rather, by nature we bow down before false gods—anything more important to us than God.

Only through faith in Jesus, Evangelicals argue, can one be accepted and produce good works pleasing to the God of Abraham, Isaac, and Jacob. And this salvation is a miraculous work, having been willed by God the Father, enacted by Christ in his life, death, and resurrection, and brought to bear in the hearts of people by the third person of the Trinity—the Holy Spirit. Evangelicals believe that salvation is a cooperative work of the three divine persons, as clearly depicted in Scripture.

In short, our own efforts and good works can't save us. Only Christ's perfect, unblemished life on earth and his atoning sacrifice upon the cross, credited to us, can. The Scriptures are clear that Jesus is the sole means of access to the God of Abraham. Jesus succinctly declares, "I am the way, the truth, and the life. No one comes to Father except through me" (John 14:6). Any attempts to

---

1. This passage is based on Pss 14:1–3, 53:1–3, and Eccl 7:20.

know God, apart from the mediatorial work of Jesus, are to no avail. Foundational to Evangelicalism is the belief that salvation is found in no one other than Christ (Acts 4:12).

Evangelicals make the counterintuitive claim that good works can't override or cancel out our sins. They can't lift us out of spiritual death or bribe God into accepting us. And, evangelical theology teaches, good works can't transform a rebel heart, which is the root of the problem.

Moreover, God wants us to truly know and love him, Evangelicals argue, instead of transactionally winning his approval on our own terms. Hence, faith in Christ is the only path to a restored relationship with him. This is indeed great news, Evangelicals claim, since sinners don't have to earn God's acceptance—he is happy to gift it to them through faith in Christ (Rom 6:23).

Once reconciled to him, good deeds flowing from faith please God, Evangelicals contend. Contrariwise, they warn, outside of a restored relationship with God, good deeds are not pleasing to him (John 14:6, 15:5–8). In the next chapter, we'll elaborate further on this unpopular idea.

6

Why Only Christians Can Please God

PREVIOUSLY, WE MADE THE outrageous claim that only Christians are able to perform good deeds that are pleasing to God. This is invariably hard to digest for unbelievers because we can observe folks of different faiths (or of no faith) doing good deeds, which naturally win our approval and appreciation.

Yet the question before us is *not* whether we or some other god can be swayed by the good deeds of non-Christians, but whether the Christian God—who claims to be the only true God—can be. And he has quite emphatically answered no to that question all throughout Scripture because the Christian God doesn't look merely at external acts like good deeds; he is intensely interested in the motives behind and circumstances around our behavior.

In Evangelical Christianity, the motives and context for good works are paramount. We can understand this because we humans also look at good deeds differently based on the motive of the good deed doer. For instance, suppose a billionaire owner of multiple car dealerships gives a million dollars from his car sales away each year to a homeless shelter. This business owner also heavily promotes his charitable giving in all of his car advertisements, e.g., "Buy a car from me, and help the homeless."

At the same time, an owner-operator of a struggling pizza shop delivers a hundred dollars worth of fresh pizzas every week to the same homeless shelter but never mentions it to anyone. Which of the two businessman is more pleasing to God? Christ clearly taught that the pizza maker deserves the greater praise (Luke 21:1–4, Matt 6:6).

One could argue: Why should motives and circumstances behind charitable gifts matter, as long as the results are good? This is because, on a relational level, motives matter greatly, and the God of Christianity is highly relational: the three persons of the Godhead live eternally in loving, selfless relationship with each other. As God's creatures, made in his image, we are intrinsically relational beings, which is why every single one of the Ten Commandments concerns either our relationship with God or with each other.

And it turns out, our motives for doing anything touch upon these relationships. Humans are not omniscient, and yet we know almost instinctively when a person is being nice to us merely because they want something from us. We call such folks "manipulators." They don't love us for who we are but for what we can do for them. It's usually also readily apparent when a person does a good deed primarily for the applause of people, rather than for its own sake. How much more is God aware of our true motives behind the "good deeds" we've done? Scripture handily notes: "A person may think their own ways are right, but the Lord weighs the heart." (Proverbs 21:2.)

Evangelicals believe that everyone is to love God authentically, not just as a means to get what we want. Jesus taught that the first and greatest commandment is to love God with all of your heart, soul, strength, and mind (Mark 12:30). We were created for this purpose: to know and love him, and to love our neighbor as we love ourselves. The biblical God wants us to have the same loving, intimate relationship with him that he had with Adam and Eve in the garden before they sinned. Evangelicals believe they were made to know and enjoy the Maker and King of the cosmos forever.

Accordingly, Evangelicals see their good works as cooperative—carried out in partnership with Christ, through the Holy Spirit who Scripture says dwells in each believer (1 Cor 12:13, Rom 8:9). If God merely demanded good deeds of his followers without guiding, empowering, and working alongside them in the process, believers would be more like employees or slaves rather than beloved sons and daughters of God. Believers, according to Evangelicals, are co-participants with God in the work of redeeming lost people and are entrusted with carrying the gospel message to the world.

Accordingly, Evangelicals insist that good works must be produced through a restored, vital relationship with God through Christ, who says, "I am the vine; you are the branches. If you remain in me and I in you, you will bear much fruit; apart from me you can do nothing" (John 15:5). So, the good deeds that are pleasing to Christ must be both preceded by conversion and facilitated by an ongoing dependence upon and empowerment through him.

THE GREATER PURPOSE OF GOOD WORKS

Some folks perform good deeds in order to negate or override sins and thereby be accepted by God. Many seem to think that God places good deeds and sins on a scale, and if the good deeds weigh more, they will go to heaven. But this is completely at odds with the theology embraced by Evangelicals; it would mean one could work his or her way into heaven and that the perfect life of Christ and his crucifixion were unnecessary.

For Evangelicals, good works can never cancel out their sins. Given the perfect righteousness God requires, one sin is enough to keep us out of heaven. After all, Adam and Eve lost the Edenic paradise with one sin—and most significantly, they surrendered their intimacy with God. This is why no one who is a sinner can earn salvation; a restored relationship with God must be received as a gift. Hence, good works are instead an expression of love and gratitude to God for that gift.

Also, the Christian's good works are intended to display the goodness and compassion of God, resulting in thanks and praise to him. Christ says, "Let your light shine before others, that they may see your good deeds and glorify your Father in heaven" (Matt 5:16).

Evangelicals will acknowledge, by the way, that any good work they do is tainted in some way. A believer may feel compelled by Christ to help an old lady cross the street. But there may be other forces at play as well—perhaps the desire for social approval, to assuage guilt, to bolster self-esteem, or to satisfy other psychological needs.

The truth is few, if any, Christian acts of mercy and service are ever done purely out of love for Christ and his glory. Fortunately, however, Christ's mercy and grace compensates for the deficiencies of these imperfect works, and Scripture supports the notion that Christians will be rewarded for them (Luke 19:15–19).

To sum up, Evangelicals trust that good works will always flow from a genuine conversion; they depend on the merit of Christ, not good deeds, for salvation. Evangelicals do good deeds out of gratitude for God's gift of salvation, not as a means of earning it. Still, Jesus does tell his disciples they will be rewarded for obeying him—something like icing on the cake of salvation—though what such rewards will look like is not altogether clear from Scripture. But these rewards—along with heaven itself—will be far greater than our minds can possibly conceive (1 Cor 2:9).

All right, we're ready to address perhaps the biggest modern complaint against Evangelical Christianity: to wit, "Why does it have to be so freakin' non-inclusive?" We'll offer a defense of salvation's singularity, straight ahead.

7

Restricted to Sinners Only

EVANGELICALS TEND TO RUFFLE some feathers when they proclaim that only Jesus can bridge the chasm of estrangement between humankind and God, and all real spiritual progress proceeds from faith in him. The notion that a person can only be saved through faith in Christ is an immovable stumbling block for many.

Given objections to the exclusivity of Christianity, it's an apt time to revisit a question every religion is trying to answer: to wit, "What is the fundamental problem afflicting humankind?" Until we answer this correctly, a solution to it—religious or secular— will remain elusive.

Humankind's big problem, as portrayed in Scripture and as understood by Evangelicals, concerns the universal state of hostilities between rebellious, sinful creatures and their holy Creator. Evangelical believers embrace the biblical teaching that we are all born as slaves to a fallen nature such that, as enumerated earlier, no one has the desire to please God, let alone even tries.

The righteous wrath of God is not an idea we take too seriously today, but genuine Christ-followers will admit that God hates and is angry at their sin and that this predicament, in light

A: Are Evangelical Christians Hypocrites?

of God's righteous commands, was a significant factor in drawing them to Jesus. Many consider this view of God primitive and have no problem replacing him with a far less threatening deity, or better—no god at all. Even some who identify as Christians take this view and dismiss hell as real. But they must ignore or reinterpret Bible passages that declare the eventuality of wrath for those who reject Christ, such as Eph 2:3 which declares, "All of us also lived among them at one time, gratifying the cravings of our flesh and following its desires and thoughts. Like the rest, we were by nature deserving of wrath."

If all have truly "sinned and fallen short of the glory of God" (Rom 3:23) as Scripture says, then everyone qualifies to be a Christian, making Christianity all-inclusive. Even vastly overqualified folks—the very worst of sinners—are welcome. Because all are invited, it should come as no surprise that the over 2.6 billion folks who identify as Christians worldwide embody all or nearly all ethnic and racial groups in the world—among those who've heard the gospel, of course.[1] (But more on the diversity of the global church a bit later.)

Yet, some will still object to the evangelical Christian idea that only one religious belief system can provide salvation and eternal life. However, it's worth considering whether God is obligated to provide a plan B or plan C, etc. for redeeming humankind from the consequences of lawbreaking.

A single path to God is unacceptable to some. But, consider someone with a life-threatening brain tumor who is informed by her doctor that only a complex and dangerous surgery can save her. That person typically does not object and say, "No worries, I'll take some aspirin and vitamins, Doc," or "Thanks, Doc, but just give me a flu shot, and I'll be fine in a couple of days."

If there's only one cure for most deadly physical diseases, why should we expect there to be more than one cure for a deadly spiritual disease?

It seems like both the physically and spiritually dying persons would be glad there is *any* cure. Faith in Christ, argue evangelical

---

1. Center for Study of Global Christianity, "Status of Global Christianity."

believers, is the only cure for sin-sick people because there's simply no other spiritual leader who even claims to have fulfilled the law of God perfectly and who can credibly assert that he raised himself back to life after dying in the stead of sinners to satisfy divine justice. Thus, Evangelicals accept Christ as the only one who can atone for their sins, as well as the only one who validated his atoning work by rising from the dead.

THE NARROW DOOR

Earlier, we emphasized that the Bible does not offer a buffet of options for being reconciled to God, nor do the overwhelming majority of religious faiths. To my knowledge, only Unitarian Universalism gives people the option of choosing their own path to God, which no doubt is a major selling point. But that idea contradicts both Old and New Testaments, where the means of atonement is clearly prescribed by God.

If there is a loving God and a heaven ruled by him, it would be odd—and not very loving—if he didn't specify the entrance requirements and communicate them clearly to us. Given the astonishing intricacy, brilliance of design, and ingenuity manifest in every single human cell, tailored precisely to each cell's specific purpose, it simply isn't credible to suggest God failed or forgot to share his intentions for the entire organism, i.e., you and me. In the biblical gospel, which even a young child can understand, Christians find unambiguous answers to the biggest questions of life, including "Why am I here?" and "What will happen after I die?"

In the United States, Universalism—or "all paths lead to God" religion—has gained more traction as Christianity has weakened. But Evangelicals see little evidence supporting the claims of Universalists. The three main branches of Christianity have changed the lives of millions, if not billions, whereas the record of faith in "all paths lead to God" has little to substantiate it as being true and transformative for either individuals or societies.

Moreover, there are no sacred texts that attest to a divine origin for Universalism, like both the Old and New Testaments which are supported by significant historical and archeological evidence over thousands of years. Also, the New Testament's accuracy is confirmed by textual analysis of thousands of first century manuscript copies; no other ancient book comes close to that level of verification. The absence of a sacred "Universalist" text that claims for itself divine authorship, as a means to establishing and confirming the truth of Universalism, suggests to Evangelicals that it is merely a human preference.

Universalism appears to be very charitable and humble, but for Evangelicals, it is actually incredibly hubristic. It's one thing to say, "I don't know if God exists," or, "I'm not sure which religion, if any, is true." But Universalists essentially say, "Whatever you believe or want to believe about God will not keep you out of heaven." Hence, Universalism rejects all exclusive claims to spiritual truth, except for one: all religions are equally legitimate, even if they largely contradict each other. Evangelicals not surprisingly view Universalism as wishful thinking.

Evangelical Christianity's assertion that it is the only way to heaven, as noted, is not unusual. As mentioned, nearly all religions claim to be exclusively true. Truth itself is, by definition, exclusive, and therefore the Christian truth that Evangelicals embrace applies to everyone. But Evangelical Christianity is exclusive only in that it excludes false ideas about who God is and how one can be reconciled to and know God; it does not exclude any person or group of people. Everyone is welcome, but its demand for repentance and adherence to the truth of Scripture naturally restricts its appeal and exerts a significant winnowing force.

8

Evangelical Christianity's Big Flaws

INDEED, IF THERE ARE inherent "flaws" that make Evangelical Christianity unpalatable for many, they are the call for repentance and the insistence on spiritual truth. Genuine faith is always paired with repentance in Scripture: the believer must agree that God's laws are right and act on this faith by turning away from sinful habits and attitudes and towards the righteous ways of Christ. The regenerative work of the Holy Spirit imparts faith to the believer and, at the very same time, sorrow over sin and a desire to turn from it.

Evangelicals recognize that folks "self-select" out of faith in Christ because they're unwilling to bear the cost of relinquishing (often long-standing) habits that Scripture deems sinful. The changes required of the believer in all areas of his or her life are enormous, though countless Evangelical converts young and old will readily testify that God was exceedingly patient and merciful as they began heeding the words of Scripture.

As noted earlier, this process is a lifetime endeavor. So, it is true that Evangelicalism is "non-inclusive" in the sense it excludes those unwilling to undergo moral transformation under the tutelage of God's Spirit, who guides, chastises, and comforts the Christian in this sanctifying work.

Is that "non-inclusiveness" unfair? Evangelicals unsurprisingly answer no. They will point to other scenarios in which human decisions dictate inclusion or non-inclusion. Athletes who compete at the Olympics are included because of their devotion and effort toward perfecting the athletic abilities bequeathed to them by nature. In a far different context, folks who are incarcerated were identified and "awarded" time in jail through their decisions to break the law.

No one seems to object to the non-inclusiveness of the Olympics and (especially) prison for good reason: we generally recognize human agency as a legitimate factor toward including or excluding people for particular roles and opportunities. This is quite different, argue Evangelicals, than when people speak of "inclusiveness" today, whereby they largely refer to facets of identity that are not chosen, such as race, gender, and disability.

In addition, many people resist or reject the gospel because they fear the reaction of family and friends and the mockery and exclusion that Evangelicals incur from unbelievers. While no one enjoys being shunned or ridiculed, evangelical believers must be willing to publicly acknowledge their faith in Christ (Matt 10:32–33).

INCLUSIVE BUT NARROW

Jesus issued numerous warnings regarding the human inclination to follow the herd, such as the following:

> Enter through the narrow gate. For wide is the gate and broad is the road that leads to destruction, and many enter through it. But small is the gate and narrow the road that leads to life, and only a few find it. (Matt 7:13)

Evangelicals are called to resist the tug of cultural values that are inconsistent with biblical mandates, which if taken alone might potentially isolate them. Yet, they are also to engage the culture they find themselves in with Christ-like behavior and the gospel. Evangelicals may certainly find these seemingly disparate callings difficult to navigate, but not impossible. In order not to be led astray by the world's value system, Evangelicals are exhorted to practice their faith through the ordinary means of prayer, worship and fellowship, Bible study, and the Protestant sacraments of baptism and communion (Jas 1:27).

Evangelicals claim to be adherents of the one true religion and the world's only means of salvation. This belief is naturally difficult for pluralistic societies to swallow—it has and continues to be viewed as an obstacle to unity and harmony. Evangelicals cling to the words of Jesus so as not to be deterred by cultural opposition, such as, "Make every effort to enter through the narrow door, because many, I tell you, will try to enter and will not be able to" (Luke 13:24).

Evangelicals are seemingly "narrow-minded" because Christ Himself claimed to be "the way, the truth, and the life" (John 14:6), and therefore the only means of salvation.

9

Evangelical Christianity Is Only for Straight, White People, Right?

THE PUBLIC PERCEPTION OF inclusion in the United States, if not the actual practice of our most prominent culture-shaping institutions, relates predominately to racial, gender, and sexual identity and thus is less associated in the public mind with socioeconomic status, religious belief, and political and ideological views. The focus here, therefore, will be on the former.

EVANGELICAL CHRISTIANITY—FOR WHITES ONLY?

In the United States, a majority (just under 59 percent) of evangelical Christians in 2015 were white, so it's natural for Americans to assume that Christianity is largely a religion for white people.[1] Yet, America is an exception to the rule globally: around the world, a whopping 84 percent of evangelical Christians in 2015 were

---

1. Center for Study of Global Christianity, "Frequently Asked Questions." See the answer to the question, "What is the ethnic makeup of world Christianity?"

non-white—which is up from 79 percent of evangelical Christians globally in 2000.[2] Hence, the Center for the Global Study of Christianity notes, "The United States is an outlier in that Evangelicalism is a majority-white movement within Christianity."[3]

Evangelicalism is largely white in America simply because whites are in the majority and because African Americans in churches that have virtually the same beliefs as white Evangelicals do not self-identify as Evangelical. Therefore, they are not included by demographers as evangelical believers in the United States. Also, the white proportion of Evangelicalism is shrinking, consistent with the decreasing overall percentage of whites nationally.[4]

It would be very hard to make the case that Evangelical Christianity is particularly appealing or somehow restricted to white people as compared to non-white folks, given that a supermajority of evangelical Christians worldwide are non-white.

Does Christianity Exclude LGBTQ+ People?

Evangelical Christians hold to the inspiration and inerrancy of Scripture because that is what the Bible claims for itself—to be the very word of God. Evangelicals view Scripture as uncompromisingly clear on the subject of sex: physical intimacy is restricted solely to the monogamous male-female marital union, to the degree that even *any thoughts or actions that lead up to or undermine* that standard are prohibited as well (Matt 5:28). It's a daunting standard for anyone, certainly including conservative Evangelical men under forty years old in the United States. A study done in 2019 found that 40 percent of men under forty had viewed pornography in that one year alone.[5]

According to evangelical belief, it's daunting because all of us—gay and straight alike—are prone from birth to sexual waywardness and distortion, simply as a consequence of our fallenness.

2. Center for Study of Global Christianity, "Frequently Asked Questions."
3. Center for Study of Global Christianity, "Frequently Asked Questions."
4. Center for Study of Global Christianity, "Frequently Asked Questions."
5. Reiss, "Conservative Christians."

A: Are Evangelical Christians Hypocrites?

"Total Depravity" is the oft-misunderstood term conveying sin's impact on all aspects of our being—including our sexuality. In short, Evangelicals say, there is a universal wayward bent affecting our sexual thoughts and behavior. Hence, it isn't that some are prone to sexual sin and some are not; it is the natural proclivity of the entire human race to violate God's standard of purity in varying ways and degrees.

Yet no one is excluded from coming to Christ and confessing the failure and frailty of his or her broken sexuality, according to Evangelicalism. Evangelicals thus desperately depend on God's promises to forgive their sexual sins as they daily struggle against and confess them, and this ongoing repentance often is a lifetime endeavor.

Many will say, even among those who profess belief in Christ, that the Bible doesn't assert a "sex within heterosexual marriage only" standard, although Evangelicals argue that the plain words of Scripture are unambiguous. Of course, Evangelicals might respond by noting it's much easier to jettison commands that forbid our strongest desires than to submit to those commands.

Earlier we emphasized that becoming an evangelical Christian is a supernatural occurrence. And if any of us who struggle in this area have the slightest hope of attaining the biblical sexual ethic, it must be supernaturally empowered. Evangelicals trust they have supernatural help on the inside: they believe the Holy Spirit will reveal to them that their sexual practices aren't what they should be and are actually harmful to others and them, as well as displeasing to God.

Given this supernatural work, new believers, gay and straight, can be delivered from the insensibility and bondage to sexual sin. The apostle Paul testifies to this reality:

> Do not be deceived: Neither the sexually immoral nor idolaters nor adulterers nor men who have sex with men nor thieves nor the greedy nor drunkards nor slanderers nor swindlers will inherit the kingdom of God. *And that is what some of you were.* But you were washed, you were sanctified, you were justified in the name of the Lord

Jesus Christ and by the Spirit of our God. (1 Cor 6:9b–11, emphasis mine)

A few blessed souls may experience nearly instantaneous and total liberation from sexual sin upon conversion. Most though, upon coming to faith in Christ, will have just begun their lifelong struggle against it. Recall that Evangelicals are people who have been changed and are changing. They have a new status as God's fully justified and cleansed children, and so are changed. And yet, Evangelicals are also just embarking on the process to becoming not just vicariously but truly righteous, a process that will be consummated only after they die.

Disregarding the Bible's prohibition of all sexual activity outside male-female married intimacy, Evangelicals claim, is to reject the goodness, truthfulness, and sovereignty of God, not only because it is commanded by Scripture but because rejecting this imperative denies what is gleaned easily enough from the complementarian nature of male and female reproductive anatomy.

So opting out of this God-ordained design, including by rejecting one's God-given gender, and engaging in anything other than married heterosexual monogamy is to spurn God, including his salvific promise to redeem us from our sexual fallenness.

Theologically liberal churches have largely departed from this standard, even to the point of blessing gay unions and ordaining gay clergy. Evangelicals, of course, strongly disagree with their positions and see these churches as denying unmistakable biblical truth.

Evangelicals contend that human inclinations regarding sexual orientation and gender identity do not override and define spiritual truth—rather, it is the other way around. Moreover, most Evangelicals would say that rejecting the traditional biblical ethic of sexuality is to make oneself a judge of Christ, who affirmed lifelong heterosexual monogamy in covenantal union, thus forfeiting any hope of deliverance and salvation (Matt 19:4).

Putting improper sexual desires—along with all other compared sins—to death is part of the Evangelical's life, making it much harder in many ways compared to the life of an agnostic or atheist. We'll elaborate more on that next.

10

How Being an Evangelical Christian Is Harder than Being an Unbeliever

KARL MARX FAMOUSLY DISPARAGED religion as an opiate for the masses. Opium, of course, delivers a short-lived euphoric escape from the struggle, failure, rejection, and disappointment in life. But in short order, it ensnares users in addiction, poverty, crime, and misery, often resulting in death.

It seems unlikely that Marx was being quite this literal, though assuredly he believed that efforts to improve the lives of the working class were hindered by workers' hope of a blissful afterlife. It seems that the faith of working-class folks hasn't undermined their economic progress, at least in capitalist societies. But is evangelical Christian faith really the anesthetic to life's painful realities that Marx claimed it to be?

Many, if not most, Evangelicals would strongly disagree. Rather than providing temporary respite from life's trials, Evangelical Christianity pushes believers to make drastic and humbling changes, which often makes life more complicated and difficult, as least in the short run. Evangelicals are to delay gratification in the here and now by denying themselves the momentary pleasures of sin, in part by steadfastly holding on to the hope of a future eternal paradise. In short, believers are called to live differently by renouncing sin and vigilantly pursuing Christlikeness for the remainder of their days.

Yet, evangelical Christians aren't likely to complain about the ephemeral difficulties after they've been born again. The gifts of forgiveness, adoption into God's family, and eternal life in heaven—and all of the other promises from Scripture to the believer—pale in comparison to the earthly struggles of following Christ, they will say. Moreover, Evangelicals typically will insist that salvation fills them with new purpose, peace, joy, and hope in spite of the new trials.

THE NEW STRUGGLE

That's not to minimize the new challenges of being an Evangelical. Often, one of the more painful aspects of being born again is the social rejection from the nonbelieving world, even from close family and friends. This is why the writers of the New Testament regularly remind believers of their glorious future, such as the apostle Paul here: "I consider that our present sufferings are not worth comparing with the glory that will be revealed in us" (Rom 8:18).

Because Evangelicals live continually under the mandate to magnify God, they must embrace becoming "slaves" to righteousness (Rom 6:18). This is why the Evangelical's life—at least in one important way—is much harder than the life of the unbeliever. In fact, being born again entails entering into a new struggle that is completely alien to non-Christians.

Evangelicals quickly discover that it's exceedingly difficult to yield to God in thought and deed for even five minutes. Thus, few if any believers come anywhere close to attaining Christ-like character in their lifetimes. The apostle Paul describes the inner battle between the old man or woman (pre-conversion) and the new man or woman (post-conversion) with naked honesty:

A: Are Evangelical Christians Hypocrites?

> So I find this law at work: Although I want to do good, evil is right there with me. For in my inner being I delight in God's law; but I see another law at work in me, waging war against the law of my mind and making me a prisoner of the law of sin at work within me. What a wretched man I am! Who will rescue me from this body that is subject to death? Thanks be to God, who delivers me through Jesus Christ our Lord! (Rom 7:21–27)

Tellingly, Paul wrote this well after his conversion. All Evangelicals are subject to this internal war, which means that every believer will vacillate to some degree between doing what pleases God and what does not. The goal, of course, is progressively to please God more often and for longer periods of time than to displease him. While the conscience of an unbeliever, largely shaped by parents and culture, weighs upon him or her in daily decision-making, the non-Christian is unable to discern God's will (1 Cor 2:14). He or she ultimately follows the allegiances of a heart untethered to God's purposes and goodness.

The internal tug-of-war within an unbeliever over a particular course of action is a fight between his or her competing priorities, none of which are to honor and glorify the one true God. These different priorities may even be between two good things—like spending more time with family or working longer hours in order to excel at a job. But faith in Christ plays no role in which priority wins out. At bottom, an unbeliever's decisions inevitably serve the perceived needs and wants of the "fallen" self, which is alienated from God, who is perfectly, eternally, and unchangeably good.

The internal tension in the believer, however, pits the "flesh" (the dethroned but still present fallen nature) against his or her new nature, which is guided and empowered by the Holy Spirit to obey God's righteous decrees. But squelching the old nature and yielding to the new nature is not automatic for the Evangelical: it requires great intentionality, effort, devotion to Scripture, prayer, and so on.

At bottom, every evangelical Christian is a work in progress—God is sculpting his followers into something beautiful. Yet, believers are not mere blocks of marble to their Creator. Unlike a human sculptor, who doesn't need the block of wood or stone to cooperate, God involves his adopted children deeply in this sculpting work, otherwise known as sanctification. In other words, God intends his people to actively participate in their own spiritual and moral growth.

God certainly is not passive in this process. For one thing, when believers stray, God, as their loving father, uses circumstances, Scripture, and conviction of wrongdoing to prompt a course correction. In short, he "spanks" his children when they behave contrary to his laws. The book of Hebrews says, "The Lord disciplines the one he loves, and he chastens everyone he accepts as his son" (Heb 12:6).

The local church also plays a vital and indispensable role in the Evangelical's spiritual growth. Believers are strengthened in faith, hope, and love through corporate worship and hearing Scripture elucidated, being encouraged and exhorted by fellow believers, participating in the sacraments, and—in a healthy church—being called to repentance when they stray from the clear instruction of Scripture.

The skeptic may find this to be small consolation. Since evangelical Christians are still sinners, isn't it reasonable to ask, "So what prevents Evangelicals from assuming attitudes and behaviors that are contrary to their marching orders and becoming people that nonbelievers might rightly fear?"

We'll get to that right up ahead.

11

Why You (Probably) Don't Need to Fear Genuine Evangelical Believers

WE'VE TALKED ABOUT THE "external" commands of God found in the Bible, which exist outside of us. Evangelicals believe Scripture is "God-breathed"—that God's words were written down by men as they were carried along by the Spirit, the third person of the Trinity. And certainly we can access these external commands by reading Scripture, thereby giving us clear instructions on how we should live (2 Pet 1:21).

But we humans are experts at ignoring divine instructions. The best selling book of all time seems also to be the most ignored one. Most houses contain several Bibles, often in pristine condition—almost as if they've never been opened! In truth, unconverted folks usually have a strong aversion to the Bible.

So God addresses this problem at conversion when he gifts to every believer his very self—in the person of the Holy Spirit—as an internal presence and guide, who draws believers to the Scriptures. Hence, Evangelicals have supernatural help and motivation "on the inside" to study and obey God's commands. The Bible itself elaborates on this gift as follows:

> What we have received is not the spirit of the world, but the Spirit who is from God, so that we may understand what God has freely given us. . . . The person without the Spirit does not accept the things that come from the Spirit of God but considers them foolishness, and cannot understand them because they are discerned only through the Spirit. (1 Cor 2:12, 14)

The supernatural work of the Holy Spirit in believers is Christ himself working in and through believers and elucidating what he's revealed in Scripture (Rom 8:9). C. S. Lewis, perhaps the greatest Christian mind of the twentieth century, helpfully explains,

> "The Christian is in a different position from other people who are trying to be good. They hope, by being good, to please God if there is one; or—if they think there is not—at least they hope to deserve approval from good men. But the Christian thinks that any good he does comes from the Christ-life inside him. He does not think God will love us because we are good, but that God will make us good because He loves us."[1]

Of course, bad habits die hard. Evangelicals must learn—through many and various trials—that they're no longer the boss of their souls. Nonetheless, the Holy Spirit prevents the truly converted from veering into unbelief and apostasy. The apostle Peter gives this assurance to true converts: "For you have been born again, not of perishable seed, but of imperishable, through the living and enduring word of God" (1 Pet 1:23).

Certainly, many who profess faith in Christ do fall away, commit heinous sins, and never return. If that Holy Spirit thingamajig presumably guards against such occurrences, why does that happen? We'll discuss that next. In your free time, go ahead and use the restroom, get a snack, walk the dog, anything. Don't mention it.

---

1. Lewis, *Mere Christianity*, 63.

12

When Evangelical Christians Don't Act Like It

Encountering a professing Evangelical who doesn't come remotely close to "walking the walk" is disconcerting. Such encounters turn unbelievers off from Christianity and besmirch the name of Christ.

You'll recall that we've been arguing that evangelical Christian conversion is a supernatural event and results in God the Holy Spirit indwelling new believers. Consequently, most genuine evangelical Christians trust they are saved forever and protected from returning to unbelief and rebellion against God (Eph 1:13–14).

The rub, of course, is that not all professing Evangelicals are "truly converted." Scripture warns that faith without works is dead, and Christ admonishes that a tree is known by its fruit (Jas 2:17, Matt 12:33). Consistently good or bad fruit are a few indicators of real conversion or merely presumption. Jesus says he will say to many, "Depart from me, I never knew you" (Matt 7:22–23). Evangelicals will largely conclude that such people were never truly converted and thus were not capable of producing the fruit of genuine repentance and faith.

As discussed previously, Christians are people who have been changed and who are changing. Though the changes in converts are rooted inwardly, they cannot help but be manifested outwardly in observable ways.

Of course for unbelievers, this may all sound like theoretical gibberish. Apart from the hard evidence of a changed life, it's too abstract. Unbelievers often need to see transformation in believers firsthand before Evangelical Christianity seems credible and real.

Seeing the effects of faith firsthand may arouse curiosity among unbelievers. The presence of joy in a new Christian, for instance, despite any improvement in his or her outward circumstances, is captivating. Another sign of transformation that skeptics can't help but notice is the love expressed between fellow believers who share little else in common beyond faith. Indeed, the apostle John writes, "By this everyone will know that you are my disciples, if you love one another" (John 13:35).

Apart from the invention of a spiritual x-ray machine, it will be hard for anyone (believers or unbelievers) to be absolutely sure if someone is a real or fake Christian because conversion happens inside and is invisible. Merely professing belief isn't a trustworthy sign of true conversion.

Beyond evidence of good or bad fruit, there are other outward signs and hints of both real and inauthentic faith. We'll get to that shortly. Before that, though, we'll make the juicy admission you've been waiting for—that Christian hypocrites really do exist! You've stuck with us this long, and now the truth is lurking right around the corner. Think of this series as one of those internet hooks like, "Celebrities you can hardly recognize these days," that keeps you clicking on the next link.

"WHAT ABOUT THE EVANGELICAL CHRISTIAN HYPOCRITES I'VE COME ACROSS?"

We've been arguing that being an Evangelical "hypocrite" is different than what unbelievers often assume. Hypocrites are folks who

A: Are Evangelical Christians Hypocrites?

impose standards on others they don't conform to themselves. Real evangelical Christians don't claim to be better than others or pretend to live up to moral laws that no one does or can. They admit to being vile sinners. Hypocrisy is pretending to be something you're not.

A truly hypocritical Evangelical may superficially display signs of being Christian without having experienced conversion by being "born again." Such folks may attend church, participate in Bible studies, engage in church charity work, and so on. But apart from being born again, also known as "regeneration," no one is saved, according to Christ. He didn't mince words in declaring the absolute necessity of this inward spiritual birth: "Truly, truly, I say to you, unless one is born again, he cannot see the kingdom of God" (John 3:3).

In short, hypocritical evangelical Christians aren't Christians at all. They're just faking it, although they may believe they've actually embraced Christ. These folks are described in Jesus' parable of the sower, in which the scriptural gospel "seed" falls on hard, rocky, or thorny ground. The gospel may even be received with great joy by these people, but since the good soil of a regenerate heart is lacking, once trouble and persecution inevitably arrives, their shallow, mirage-like "faith" vanishes (Mark 4:3–20).

It is only after a supernatural tilling of the heart's soil that people will respond favorably to the gospel. Without it, a person who professes faith in Christ will eventually forsake him, or perhaps find comfort in a dead church that is blind to or silent about the necessity of conversion.

As a practical matter, it's impossible to live the Christian life apart from this transformational and invisible work on the inside. It's hard enough to follow and obey Jesus after being born again. The unconverted person who claims to be an evangelical Christian may appear to conform outwardly to Christianity, but he or she will be spiritually blind, undiscerning, and unable to hear and respond to God's leadership.

Genuine evangelical believers fall into grievous sin too. But it's often the case that big scandals attributed to Evangelicals are actually traceable to fake Christians—even, and perhaps especially, disingenuous clergy (paging Joel Osteen and other prosperity gospel evangelists[1]).

This all may sound sneakily "convenient." When professing Evangelicals commit heinous sins, there's an escape hatch: "Hey," the church claims, "it's obvious they weren't Christians after all." So, evangelical Christians and Christianity itself aren't to blame for blatant public sins. "That's pretty slick," concludes the skeptic.

We'll try our best to respond to that criticism in our next installment. Maybe it's a cop-out. Or perhaps it's totally predictable, based on what Christ taught.

---

1. See Ligonier Ministries, "What Is the Prosperity Gospel?" for a helpful explanation of the prosperity gospel.

13

Why Are There So Many Fake Christians?

WE LAST NOTED THAT the shameful shenanigans of fake evangelical believers often get attributed to Evangelicalism. Faithful Evangelicals may point out, "That poser was never a Christian in the first place! Don't blame it on us!" To skeptics, that sounds mighty convenient—like something comedian Dana Carvey's irrepressible "Church Lady" of *Saturday Night Live* would instantly recognize as a ploy straight out of Lucifer's playbook.

But there are compelling reasons why it shouldn't be assumed Evangelicalism is to be blamed for the bad acts of fake evangelical Christians. It has to do with why and how people become Evangelicals in the first place.

Here's the thing: Christianity has significant intellectual and historical credibility, it meets fundamental human needs, and it gives a reassuring answer to the biggest question of all—what happens after we die? For those reasons alone, Christianity naturally draws people of different stripes. Add to all that the pristine beauty of the TV preacher and his wife, the angelic singing of the choir, and the promises of financial security and perfect health every

Sunday morning on TV, and you have an irresistible toxic brew of "Salvation Lite."

Accordingly, many Evangelicals profess faith in Christ even when the supernatural work of spiritual birth ("regeneration") is absent. In the parable of the sower, discussed earlier, Jesus makes it clear that a large number of folks will eventually walk away from faith in Christ, particularly when the they face difficulty or opposition. Jesus says they fall away because they have no root—which we can reasonably surmise is the new birth resulting in the inward presence of God himself (Eph 4:20–24).

This tendency of people to receive the gospel with joy but to fall away when trouble arises is why Jesus counsels prospective believers to "count the cost" before deciding to follow Christ (Luke 14:28–30). As we belabored earlier, salvation is free. However, being a disciple of Christ is not, which is not contradictory but certainly paradoxical.

Evangelicals believe that adoption into the eternal family of God comes purely as an act of grace. This gift of salvation, however, is not merely a ticket to heaven. Evangelicals believe that this grace not only bestows eternal life, it also transforms a rebel heart into one that wants to love and please God. True conversion always results in a desire to follow and serve Christ.

Yet the good works of discipleship most definitely are not automatic; they require great sacrifice on the part of the believer, even while being mysteriously animated by the Holy Spirit. Again, this may seem at odds with the idea of salvation as an unearned gift. But it is a paradox, not a contradiction, pointing to the reality that while justification and sanctification are supernaturally enabled in different ways, both also involve a response from the prospective convert.

Sanctification entails a believer's strenuous effort in obedience to and cooperation with God. Indeed, the apostle Paul exhorts believers to "continue to work out your salvation with fear and trembling, for it is God who works in you to will and to act in order to fulfill his good purpose" (Phil 2:13). So, it is both a work of God and of man.

A: Are Evangelical Christians Hypocrites?

DISTINGUISHING REAL FROM FAKE

Christ was totally up-front with the "downsides" of following him. This was both honest and compassionate: it's better for folks to know sooner rather than later if they really belong to him or are only after a "ticket to heaven." He didn't want anyone to be fooled on an issue as important as their eternal standing with God.

That's why Evangelicals emphasize the need to be born again—especially since in many non-evangelical churches today, you'll never be challenged this way. In truth, the call of Jesus is so daunting that when even devoted evangelical Christians do a self-assessment, they may well ask themselves, "Am I really a Christian—have I really been changed?" It's good for converts and presumed converts to ask themselves this question, and in itself is typically a sign of genuine belief.

Contrarily, fake believers may complacently roll along without ever truly examining the genuineness of their faith and thereby never seeing their need for the new birth, faith, and repentance. Evangelicals believe that any profession of faith is presumptuous when it isn't accompanied by repentance.

Evangelicals are to seek assurance that their faith is real. The New Testament tells believers "to confirm your calling and election" (2 Pet 1:10), and Jesus counsels that "anyone who chooses to do the will of God will find out whether my teaching comes from God or whether I speak on my own" (John 7:17). Evangelicals trust that God "shows up" when they exercise faith, confirming his love and salvation.

THE ONLY REAL CHRISTIANS ARE INVISIBLE

We've been confronting the reality that many professing evangelical Christians are not saved at all. They came for the benefits without heeding the call to repentance. They may have gone forward when summoned by an evangelical preacher and recited a salvation prayer spoken by the preacher. Unfortunately, responding to an altar call may be a purely emotional response, unaccompanied by an invisible conversion inside. Such responses lack the staying power of genuine faith empowered by the indwelling Spirit. Hence, when the inevitable rejection and hardship associated with following Christ appear, unconverted "believers" often head for the exits.

Let's paraphrase one of the less-beloved promises to believers in Scripture: "You will be persecuted!" (2 Tim 3:12). In America, that typically only amounts to social derision and exclusion, though it may also result in employment discrimination and other financial harm. In less tolerant countries, where Christian expression may be restricted or altogether banned, evangelical believers may get blessed with jail, beatings, and even murder. For instance, the approximately one hundred million Christians in China are facing increasing persecution in the form of church demolitions, disappearing pastors and priests, imprisonment, and harassment.[1]

Unconverted "evangelical Christians" may also tire of Christ's call to holiness: the need to continually confess and repent of their sins, and the challenges of resting and depending completely on God's direction and grace. Hence, attrition and apathy among folks who once embraced and followed Christ is high, which outsiders may view as a defect in Christianity itself.[2] Yet Christ warned of this reality and issued the scary admonition that he would turn away many at the final judgement with the terrifying words, "I never knew you" (Matt 7:23).

A more sinister brand of inauthentic or hypocritical Christianity is practiced by false teachers, who the apostle Peter says are typically motivated by greed. Peter further tells us that "many will follow their depraved conduct and will bring the way of truth into disrepute" (2 Pet 2:2). Thus, the great apostle makes it clear that the seductive lies of these false teachers, and those who are led astray by them, will result in many becoming suspicious of and even hostile to Christianity. Sadly, there are many "donate to me and get rich" preachers, who are described in Scripture as "ravenous wolves" (Matt 7:15).

1. Chalufour, "Boom of Christianity"; Mauro, "Christian Persecution in China."

2. Clark, "Survey Shows."

A: Are Evangelical Christians Hypocrites?

There is no dearth of these false teachers and prophets, says the Bible. These manipulators opened up shop upon Christ's resurrection and ascension, prompting the apostle John to warn that "many false prophets have gone out into the world" (1 John 4:1). As a result, there are currently large nonorthodox sects—like Mormonism, Jehovah's Witnesses, and the aforementioned "prosperity gospel" groups—that peddle their false gospel under the pretense of Christianity.

It's also why the church has always recognized the difference between the visible and invisible church. The visible church is comprised of all who fill the pews on Sunday while the invisible church is made of the truly converted, "born-again" believers, whom Scripture calls "the body of Christ" (John 3:3, 1 Cor 12:27).

Consequently, an important task of evangelical clergy is to continually underscore the gospel in worship services so that the unconverted in their midst might come to genuine faith. And both clergy and lay leaders are duty bound to know their parishioners well enough to discern the state of each person's soul so that they may personally engage the unconverted regarding their need for salvation. Sadly, even some evangelical churches fall short in this crucial task.

While there's no foolproof methodology of knowing whether a person is truly saved, there are nonetheless plenty of signs that make genuine faith reasonably detectable. We'll look at those up ahead.

14

How Can You Tell if Someone's Truly Saved?

MANY TIMES, SKEPTICS WILL observe the bad fruit from an unconverted "Evangelical" and conclude that Christianity itself is at fault. In life generally, more often than not, "the proof is in the pudding," so that's understandable. Unfortunately, not all pudding is even pudding, which you certainly know if you've ever tried store-bought "pudding" snacks. There are a few key clues, however, in discerning the real from the fake Evangelical.

THE TELLS OF GENUINE BELIEF

The first and most important way of figuring out whether someone is a Christian or not is—sorry to have to bring this distasteful word up—doctrinal. Evangelical Christians believe in a God of truth (John 14:6). He not only is the source of all truth but he is truth itself. As noted, Evangelicals put their trust in the inerrant truth of his written revelation: the Bible.

A: Are Evangelical Christians Hypocrites?

Evangelical faith is not in vague ideas about God but in what he has explicitly and substantively revealed about himself in Scripture, including his moral laws and the way of salvation. The genuine evangelical believer is one who knows, assents, and trusts in "God's word"—holy Scripture, which Evangelicals accept as complete in supplying all that is needed for faith and practice (2 Tim 3:15). Certainly, a first step toward becoming a Christian is to believe Christ's promises of forgiveness and eternal life in Scripture, as well as his warnings about the seriousness of sin and of hell for the unrepentant.

Christians worldwide—not just Evangelicals—agree on a number of basic biblical truths. They include things like the divinity and humanity of Christ, the tripersonal nature of God, Christ's substitutionary atonement on the cross, his resurrection, and so on. C. S. Lewis referred to these basic, essential truths as "mere Christianity" in his eponymously titled book. Of course, there is disagreement on the finer (not to be construed as "insignificant") points of theology among the various Christian denominations, but agreement on the major ones provides for a basic doctrinal test.

In other words, if anyone denies any of these essential truths, he or she is not a Christian. Our purpose here is not to lay out these truths in their entirety. Lewis's *Mere Christianity* and many similar books lay out the doctrinal foundations of Christian orthodoxy. By the way, fully comprehending these truths is not required—it's safe to say no one has a complete and perfect grasp of them.

Evangelical Christians believe them because God, who cannot lie, has clearly revealed them in Scripture (Heb 6:18). They form, then, the doctrinal boundaries of Christianity and thus are enormously helpful in discerning who is a Christian, as well as which churches are truly Christian. Of course, if you want to use this test, you'll need to be acquainted with them yourself.

BEHAVIORAL HINTS

If one looks closely enough, the genuine evangelical believer can often be discerned from the fake. As noted previously, Christ taught that a tree is known by its fruit. Believers will bear good fruit while the fruit of the unconverted "Christian" ultimately will prove to be rotten. In each case, though, it may take some time either for the fruit to ripen into sweetness or else to be exposed as decorative, superficial, and rancid. The lives of many genuine Christians will be unimpressive, especially in the infancy of their faith journey, unless you know their backstory and what they might otherwise have been had Christ not redeemed them.

Early on, though, there are some telltale signs. For one thing, genuine evangelical believers will fail frequently, but they will also admit their failures and continually seek to repent of them. On the other hand, fake Evangelicals are less willing to admit their weaknesses or confess their wrongs. They may still fool some folks with false humility and good works for show, belying the true state of their hearts.

In short, although truly repentant Evangelicals are never done with sin, they're also never done with repenting of it. They live, as it has often been expressed, at the foot of the cross. Non-Christians may witness Evangelicals sinning, but if they also observe remorse and amends being made, they won't necessarily deduce hypocrisy.

Also, sincere evangelical believers will readily admit they've checked themselves into a sin hospital (the church), and are being treated by the only effective sin doctor (Jesus). For many fake Christians, their association with the church isn't rooted in the need for forgiveness, but the desire for social approval.

Most unregenerate evangelical church attenders are also reluctant to acknowledge their "faith" in Christ publicly. There is no such thing as "closet Christianity," according to Jesus. He says,

> Whoever acknowledges me before others, I will also acknowledge before my Father in heaven. But whoever disowns me before others, I will disown before my Father in heaven. (Matt 10:32–33)

In addition, as authentic Evangelicals grow spiritually, so will their awareness of their own sinfulness, even though ironically they sin less. Moreover, evangelical believers realize that any good fruit they produce never occurs independently of God's Spirit within them. "I am the vine; you are the branches. If you remain in me and I in you, you will bear much fruit; apart from me you can do nothing," Christ declared (John 15:5). Accordingly, true believers are less confident in their own goodness and thereby humbler than before they believed. The fake Christian will not experience this inner transformation.

Of course, learning to yield to God's Spirit and to live out one's new identity as a child of God isn't instantaneous. It's a slow, often painstaking, and rocky ride that will last a lifetime. No one achieves sinlessness before dying, and infinitesimally few come anywhere close.

Nonetheless, Evangelicals trust that there will be progress, and Scripture promises that genuine believers will cross the finish line—upon their death or Christ's return—by staying true to their faith in him (Phil 1:6). Moreover, Evangelicals are confident that, once in heaven, their battle with sin will be over. These evangelical believers embrace the scriptural promise that they will be transformed "in the twinkling of an eye," becoming perfectly righteous and therefore forever free from sin—and the accusation of hypocrisy (1 Cor 15:51–52).

B

Don't Bite the Book That Feeds You

(Note: Evangelicals contend that developing a relationship with your Creator is a bit different than getting to know a new neighbor, coworker, or classmate. Duh! But there are some similarities. For instance, openness to and tolerance for differences, not to mention humility and sincerity, can help grease the relational skids. Evangelical Christians believe that God reveals himself through Scripture in tangible ways, as long as the reader observes some basic commonsense guidelines.)

INTRODUCTION

IF ANYONE DESIRES TO know who God is and what he is like, evangelical Christians point to his dual self-revelation: nature and the Bible. Nature is God's twenty-four seven beacon to the entire human race; no one can avoid it, and so it is exhibit A in the case against those who claim ignorance of God. At the same time, nature's communication to us is largely passive, outside of lightning strikes, tornadoes, and other displays that redirect our thoughts to the metaphysical.

Those predisposed against belief in a supernatural creator can convince themselves—with small encouragement—that the intricacy, beauty, and intelligence pervading nature is purely accidental. Indeed, nature for some may have the appearance of randomness, but under a microscope its ingenious design and mind-boggling complexity are impossible to deny.

Also, nature's testimony to God's existence is limited in scope—while it provides important clues to God's character, it pales in comparison to the detailed and comprehensive disclosure of God in holy Scripture. To really know God, then, we must actively engage Scripture with our minds and hearts. We will not apprehend God in the Bible—just as we won't apprehend the meaning of any book—until and unless we permit (and even invite) the author to speak his or her unique message to us.

Jesus often prefaced his teaching by saying, "Whoever has ears, let them hear" (Matt 11:15). By this metaphor, in which he likens hearing to spiritual receptivity, he challenges his audience's readiness to consider something completely different from what they were used to hearing from their spiritual masters. He was under no illusion that everyone was prepared, morally and spiritually, to receive his message, most especially the "spiritual masters"!

A genuine encounter with God, Evangelicals say, is preconditioned by one's openness to spiritual truth and sincerity in seeking him. The wrong approach can easily sabotage one's apprehension of God and doom the pursuit of him from the outset. God does not operate within cultures and throughout history as we might expect or assume, and thus we must be at least as tolerant and open-minded in approaching God as is demanded in twenty-first-century America of differing lifestyles. With that in mind, we hereby propose a few guidelines on cultivating "ears to hear."

DON'T OFF-LOAD THE HEAVY LIFTING TO THIRD-PARTY CYNICS

Too often, folks have negative impressions of the Bible not due to their own reading but because of what has been conveyed to them by third-party Bible "experts"—including and perhaps especially folks with deep animus to Scripture. We all bring our own biases and preconceptions to Scripture, but at least they're our own. Any additional baggage from self-anointed YouTube Bible "scholars" is just as likely to obfuscate as elucidate.

So, should you "take up and read," as St. Augustine famously did upon the inadvertent prompting of children chanting that phrase in Latin, "*Tolle Lege*," we strongly recommend engaging Scripture firsthand, at least prior to resorting to third-party commentary.[1]

GO WOKE, WIND UP SPIRITUALLY BROKE

The profundities of Scripture are unlikely to be unlocked through the lens of twenty-first-century wokeness. Examining Scripture in light of woke sensibilities tends to result in finger-wagging at God and concluding that he falls miserably short of one's own superior moral standards.

Consider that, for all your great learning and insight, you still just emerged from the womb less than a nanosecond ago relative to eternity, or as compared to evolutionary biology's purported timeline. Moreover, judging God and Scripture based on twenty-first-century standards ignores major social and political advances—significantly driven by biblical ethics and championed by committed Christians, we'd argue—since the premodern world of antiquity. Of course, Christians have failed badly at times throughout history, but overall Christianity has contributed mightily to human dignity and rights.

Indeed, even agnostic historians recognize this. In his article "Atheists in Praise of Christianity," Jonathan Van Maren observes that unbelieving scholars are acknowledging that Christianity is

---

1. Augustine, *Confessions* 8.12.

integral to liberal Western ethics. Respected historian Tom Holland documents this reality in his book, *Dominion: How the Christian Revolution Remade the World*. In discussing the book, Jonathan Van Maren details how, according to Holland, Christianity shaped Western mores and thought. Van Maren recounts Holland's description of the ancient world as being horrifically cruel in how it treated the weakest and poorest, particularly unwanted newborns, slaves, and women. Infanticide and the economic, physical, and sexual exploitation of the most vulnerable were commonplace in antiquity.

Van Maren explains why and how that changed:

> How did we get from there to here? It was Christianity, Holland writes. Christianity revolutionized sex and marriage, demanding that men control themselves and prohibiting all forms of rape. Christianity confined sexuality within monogamy. (It is ironic, Holland notes, that these are now the very standards for which Christianity is derided.) Christianity elevated women. In short, Christianity utterly transformed the world.[2]

Hence, we could not even conceive of the world we live in apart from Christ's life, death, and resurrection, Holland contends. Indeed, the liberal West would not have been birthed absent the person and work of Jesus Christ. Western laws and values protecting individual rights flow directly from Christianity; moreover, Holland argues these same values ultimately underpin "woke" ethics. Hence, he submits, wokeness itself could never have arisen apart from Christianity.

Today's woke leaders seem blissfully unaware that Christianity has been a powerful impetus for positive social change. The failure to see that our current views of human rights didn't just emerge from the ether but are deeply indebted to Judeo-Christian morality should make "woke-sters" pause before insisting Scripture and devout Christians have no place in the public sphere.

2. Van Maren, "Atheists."

The Example of Slavery

Sadly, evangelical Christians are culpable for cooperating with and participating in the enslavement of kidnapped African men and women during the time of slavery in America. Members of evangelical churches, largely in the South, either owned slaves themselves, implicitly supported slavery, or otherwise failed to oppose the horrific practices of African slavery. Moreover, evangelical leaders and churches justified owning slaves by ignoring or misinterpreting unambiguous Scriptures; they neither condemned chattel slavery or its pernicious source: the kidnapping and exceedingly cruel transport of African men and women on transatlantic ships. In his apologetic book, *The Reason for God*, the late evangelical pastor Tim Keller writes, "A deep stain on Christian history is the African slave trade."[3]

Certainly, some of those who held slaves or supported slavery were not genuinely Christian, although they likely assumed so because nearly all Southern whites living at this time would have identified as Christian. But merely living in a culture dominated by Christians isn't a proxy for genuine faith. Nonetheless, many genuine believers undeniably rationalized, tolerated, and even participated in the enslavement of African Americans. The very fact that the dehumanization of chattel slaves could occur in a culture steeped in Christianity seems unfathomable in view of Scripture's exhortations against this cruel debasement of God's image-bearers.

It was both horribly wrong and evil, as it starkly contradicts Scripture's succinct and unmistakable laws. Indeed, the Bible's teaching on slavery totally repudiates the practices of kidnapping and enslaving people based on race and ethnicity and motivated by greed.

---

3. Keller, *Reason for God*, 64.

Part One: What Evangelicals Believe

Slavery in the Old Testament

In the Old Testament, slavery was strictly regulated, and thereby it departs diametrically from the deeply embedded institution that was practiced in most ancient societies. God's commands radically reconfigured and repurposed it to reflect his concern for the poor and the alien.

Sound far-fetched? Consider the following:

- In the Old Testament Scriptures, kidnapping ("man-stealing") and trafficking in slaves are capital offenses. African slave traders by law would have been stoned to death had they lived in ancient Israel (Exod 21:16).[4]

- Slavery among Israelites in Scripture was voluntary and designed to meet the needs of the poor and those in debt (Lev 25:47–49).

- Israelite slavery primarily is a kind of temporary indentured servitude, limited in duration to six years regardless of whether a slave had paid off a debt (Exod 21:2).

- Biblical slavery was a kind of safety net for indigent persons long before the advent of the welfare state. Israeli slaves were never owned by their masters and were protected by law against physical abuse (Exod 21:26–27).

- Both Hebrew and foreign slaves were to be loved by their masters and by all Israelites. Israel's history as an enslaved people in Egypt is explicitly cited in Scripture as the key rational for treating slaves with dignity and compassion (Lev 19:33–34).

- Runaway slaves were guaranteed safe harbor—the law forbade anyone from returning a slave to a master he or she had run away from (Deut 23:15–16).

The prohibition against returning slaves did not mean that a person who had "sold" themselves into slavery could not be

---

4. Got Questions, "Bible Condone Slavery?"

apprehended if they had debt remaining—like any other debtor, they could be required to fulfill their debt obligation.[5] But after six years, as noted, they'd be released whether or not the debt was fully satisfied.

While foreign slaves in Israel did not automatically become free after six years, given their inability to purchase land in Israel apart from conversion, the general principles guaranteeing the humane treatment of Israeli slaves applied to foreign slaves as well.[6] Again, Scripture emphasizes the rationale for this unusual concern and protection which resonated strongly with the people of ancient Israel:

> When a foreigner resides among you in your land, do not mistreat them. The foreigner residing among you must be treated as your native-born. Love them as yourself, for you were foreigners in Egypt. I am the Lord your God. (Lev 19:33–34)

How important was it that Israelites treat aliens with great dignity? One scholar notes,

> God repeatedly expresses great concern for the *orphan*, the *widow*, and the *alien*—the most vulnerable in Israelite society. In fact, the Lord reminds the Israelites *three dozen times* to care for the "alien," and no doubt this includes *foreign* servants.[7]

Moreover, as stated above, Israelites were explicitly commanded not to return a foreign slave that ran away from its owner. The practice of slavery, in most or all other contexts, imposes severe penalties on runaway slaves and those that harbor them. Contrarily, God commanded the Israelites that

> if a slave has taken refuge with you, do not hand them over to their master. Let them live among you wherever they like and in whatever town they choose. Do not oppress them. (Deut 23:15–16)

---

5. Compelling Truth, "Slavery Allowed in the Old Testament?"
6. Compelling Truth, "Slavery Allowed in the Old Testament?"
7. Copan, "Servitude."

If slaves can leave a household without fear of punishment or return, or alternatively freely choose to join that household permanently as a servant (Exod 21:6), it is reasonable to question whether it is proper to call them slaves at all.[8] Slaves, by definition, lack such freedom of movement and often any lawful rights protecting them from abuse.

At bottom, the slavery permitted by God among Israelites in the Old Testament transformed the slavery of the ancient world from a vehicle purely for economic gain that was highly susceptible to cruel oppression, into a means of sustenance and protection of the poor and the alien.

Slavery in the New Testament

Slavery was widespread throughout the Roman Empire in the period of and well after Christ's birth. While estimates differ, it appears that as many as 30 percent of the population under Roman rule were slaves.[9] Roman slavery took many different forms: chattel slavery, debt bondage, and indentured servanthood, along with slavery resulting from foreign conquest. Thus, slavery varied widely as regards work expectations and living conditions.[10]

The New Testament doesn't include a proclamation universally denouncing and barring slavery,[11] as if such an order would compel owners and society to liberate slaves and to dismantle its legal apparatus, apart from changed hearts and a moral awakening by means of conversion and faith.

The four Gospels of the New Testament are relentlessly focused on the person and work of Christ and his provision for what Evangelicals see as humankind's greatest need: forgiveness by and reconciliation with God. Evangelicals maintain that hope

---

8. Copan, Reasonable Faith.
9. Compelling Truth, "Slavery Allowed in the New Testament?"
10. Compelling Truth, "Slavery Allowed in the New Testament?"
11. Compelling Truth, "Slavery Allowed in the New Testament?"

for cultural and societal change is ultimately futile apart from individual reconciliation with God.

Surely, Christ's teaching has profound import for all human relationships, including the relationships between slaves and slaveholders. For instance, Christ's parable of the good Samaritan universalizes the meaning of "neighbor," i.e., those we are to love selflessly. He insists we not only are to love folks in our families, cultures, and churches, but we are to love even those we despise and consider beneath us, as slaveholders often might feel toward slaves.

The apostle Paul, the writer of most of the New Testament outside of the Gospels, deals more directly with slaves and their owners, ultimately laying the moral and spiritual groundwork for slavery's end.[12] For instance, Paul implores believers to honor the dignity of slaves and to love all people. Accordingly, in Galatians, he exhorts Christians on the spiritual equality of slaves and owners:

> For you are all children of God through faith in Christ Jesus. And all who have been united with Christ in baptism have put on Christ, like putting on new clothes. There is no longer Jew or Gentile, slave or free, male and female. For you are all one in Christ Jesus. (Gal 3:26–28)

Evangelical Efforts to End Slavery

While in no way absolving Evangelicals for their rol in the deplorable history of African slavery, it is also true that many Evangelicals initiated and successfully led efforts in America and Great Britain to end the African slave trade and eventually slavery itself, since the Bible clearly condemns the vicious cruelty and oppression inflicted on slaves by African slave traders and owners. Tim Keller observes,

> Christians began to work for the abolition [of slavery] not because of some general understanding of human rights, but because they saw it as violating the will of God.... [Evangelical] Christian activists such as William

---

12. Condone Slavery, Pursuing God.

Wilberforce in Great Britain, John Woolman in America, and many, many others devoted their entire lives, in the name of Christ, to ending slavery.[13]

Ultimately, evangelical leaders and churches were deeply convicted by the biblical teachings contradicting the practice of slavery in the United States. It was not any deficiencies in Scripture but the unfaithfulness of Christians who failed to heed the Bible that contributed to the cruelty of slavery.

In the larger context of human history, Christianity has been a powerful force in eradicating slavery. As noted, abolishment of the despicable practices of chattel slavery in the United States and England was organized and championed by Christians.[14] Similarly, the dignity and rights of women, widows, and preborn and newly born babies have been significantly advanced in the West and globally by Christians.[15]

THE EXCLUSIVITY BUGABOO

In the pluralistic West, aversion to evangelical insistence on "one true God" is endemic. Our democratic mindset as regards governance is partially to blame. The American Constitution, a transcendent breakthrough in governmental architecture, guarantees the right to worship or not to worship the god(s) of our choosing, which most will agree is wonderful. But Evangelicals will argue that it's quite a leap to infer that is also God's policy. It may seem charitable to say that all religious paths lead to the same mountaintop, but that approach ends up sacrificing spiritual truth on the altar of niceness.

It actually is quite presumptuous to assume God accepts any beliefs or the lack thereof regarding his nature and ways to worship him. In pagan antiquity, the "Shema" pronouncement—"Hear, O

---

13. Keller, *Reason for God*, 67.

14. Keller, *Reason for God*, 64–65. See also James, "Tracing Christianity's Impact."

15. James, "How Christianity Transformed."

Israel: The Lord our God, the Lord is one" (Deut 6:4)—was truly groundbreaking as a frontal attack on the worship of multiple gods that was the existing and unchallenged norm. Evangelicals understand God as self-existent, omnipotent, omniscient, immutable, and eternal, and He isn't okay with his creatures playing around with cheap counterfeits. He is a jealous God who wired us to worship him alone in spirit and truth (John 4:24). Putting one's faith in anything other than the one, true God, according to Evangelicals, is offensive to God and has a history of dragging people into detestable and dehumanizing idolatry, as the Bible warns repeatedly.

Evangelical Christianity, like pretty much every other religion, proposes a single path to God. The existence of a single, all-powerful God isn't forbidden by logic. Logic only forbids the existence of more than one omnipotent sovereign of the universe—a problem multiculturalists don't seem to have noticed.

In his work *The Reason for God*, the late evangelical pastor Tim Keller sheds light on how skeptics who recoil at exclusive religious claims actually are believers in their own singular "faith":

> Skeptics believe that *any* exclusive claims to a superior knowledge of spiritual reality cannot be true. But this objection is itself a religious belief. It assumes God is unknowable, or that God is loving but not wrathful, or that God is an impersonal force rather than a person who speaks in Scripture. All of these are unprovable faith assumptions. In addition, their proponents believe they have a superior way to view things. They believe the world would be a better place if everyone dropped the traditional religions' views of God and truth and adopted theirs. Therefore, their view is also an exclusive claim about the nature of spiritual reality. If all such views are to be discouraged, this one should be as well.[16]

If you approach the evangelical belief in "one God" with a hardened conviction that there cannot possibly be one true religion, you've already embraced a religious belief—one for which there exists very little or no evidence. Accordingly, as soon as you encounter

---

16. Keller, *Reason for God*, 12–13; emphasis in original.

the Shema, you'll conclude, "Well, this God isn't for me," because he contradicts your preexisting faith in a God who would never exclude anyone based on how they define and worship him. Evangelicalism insists that God must be approached with humility and reverence, not with preconceived notions of who he "should" be.

At bottom, Evangelicals argue that the identity and nature of God is not up to us. We may wish God were many things. It's quite common today for people to reject Evangelicalism solely because it allows for only one way to God. Unfortunately, when we project our own wishes and beliefs onto the Almighty, we end up creating God in our own image.

"YOUR FAMILY AND CULTURE MADE YOU A CHRISTIAN!"

If you reject Evangelical Christianity's exclusivity because it is the dominant system of belief in your culture, as that presumably would encourage you to look down upon non-Christian cultures, you won't have avoided the charge of ethnocentrism. Tim Keller again helpfully explains why:

> Most non-Western cultures have no problem saying that their culture and religion is the best. The idea that it is wrong to do so is deeply rooted in Western traditions of self-criticism and individualism. To charge others with the "sin" of ethnocentrism is really a way of saying, "Our culture's approach to other cultures is superior to yours." We are then doing the very thing we forbid others to do.[17]

In short, patronizing other cultures by virtue of a relativistic Western mindset is no less ethnocentric than outright disagreeing with the religious views of such cultures.

If you fear ethnocentrism, you may also feel that confidence in the Bible is purely the result of social conditioning. The thinking goes, "Naturally, people who grow up in devout evangelical families and in countries where Evangelicalism is a popular religion,

---

17. Keller, *Reason for God*, 12.

like America, are much more likely to become Bible-believing Christians, apart from whether it's true or not."

That's a far more tenuous argument today as Evangelicalism has fallen into disfavor in America and other Western cultures where church attendance and the Bible's cultural relevance have been on a steep downward trajectory. If you want to be part of the smart crowd in America, it's probably best to keep your biblical faith on the down-low.

While Christianity is declining here, though, it is growing explosively in predominantly non-Christian areas of the world like Africa and Asia. It is not uncommon in these places for converts to Christianity to face rejection, disapproval, and even brutal persecution from their own cultures, and even within their own families. If Christian faith is merely an effect of social conditioning, these dangerous and costly conversions to Christianity are rather curious.

Nonetheless, it's certainly true that Evangelicalism is often transmitted through families and culture. But isn't atheism also passed on that way? Sociobiologists would go even further and contend that religion is not really chosen at all; instead, it's programmed into our DNA as an inherited trait, just like hair and skin color.[18] Of course, that would make unbelief—atheism—part of one's genetic inheritance, too.

But neither theory—whether one believes faith is purely the product of social conditioning or solely the result of genetic transmission, or some combination thereof—comes anywhere close to debunking Evangelicalism. Each has significant evidential and logical flaws. Moreover, adopting any of these theories would mean our "freethinking" atheist friends may not be quite as "freethinking" as they'd like to believe, and also would make their antagonism to theism quite predictable.

---

18. Mohler, "God Gene."

DON'T ASSUME GRACE AND JUDGMENT CAN'T COEXIST

Many refrain from reading the Old Testament because of a misimpression that it is all about God's wrath and devoid of any mercy and grace. Some folks reject a God of judgment out of hand, without considering whether a God who overlooked unspeakable evil would be worth knowing and worshiping.

The evil that precipitates God's judgement in the Old Testament—like the horror of child sacrifice—certainly merits wrath. Moreover, the divine justice in the Old Testament typically is preceded by God's repeated warnings and patient forbearance, Evangelicals argue.

Indeed, Evangelicals do not view judgement in the Bible as capricious or willy-nilly, but as God's righteous response to the unrelenting evil of humankind. Noah's flood is precipitated by this pronouncement:

> The Lord saw how great the wickedness of the human race had become on the earth, and that every inclination of the thoughts of the human heart was only evil all the time. (Gen 6:5)

Contrary to the critics' portrayal of God as an angry despot, for many Evangelicals what is most shocking when first encountering the Old Testament, such as the book of Genesis, is the ridiculous and nearly offensive outpouring of grace to scoundrels. For instance, Jacob, a serial trickster and manipulator, nonetheless continually reaps the benefits of God's long-suffering and exorbitant favor.

On one such occasion, two of Jacob's sons (chips off the old blockhead) use deceit to avenge the rape of their sister, Dinah, by the prince of a small Canaanite tribe. They exact vengeance by slaughtering all the men in this tribe and then abscond with the tribe's wives, children, animals, and possessions. Jacob, the head of this extraordinarily dysfunctional clan, says little in response to the rape of his only daughter and appears to be primarily concerned with how the sons' murderous revenge might antagonize other tribes against them (Gen 34). It is a monumental failure of fatherly responsibility and love. Yet, God keeps his promises to greatly bless Jacob and his unruly family, even while severely chastening their waywardness.

The Old Testament repeatedly tells us that God is "compassionate and gracious, slow to anger, and abounding in lovingkindness and truth" (Exod 34:6). And God amply demonstrates this overflowing love toward his stubbornly rebellious children, the nation of Israel, throughout the Old Testament Scriptures—the very same love that Evangelicals believe they reap through faith in Christ. Evangelicals similarly see in the Old Testament how God's long-suffering toward their own rebellious ways was shown to the Israelites.

Abraham has a habit of lying to wriggle out of tough spots. Noah's a drunkard. David is an adulterer and murderer. Time and again, these "heroes" of Scripture screw up royally—and not just before God reveals himself to them but well after they are acquainted with his moral perfection and expectations. Spiritual progress by the Old Testament saints and the nation of Israel frequently seems to be one step forward and two back, as is the case with Evangelicals, most believers will admit.

Evangelicals do not see a disconnect between the Old and New Testaments. Rather, Evangelicals recognize that the Old Testament dispenses not only law and judgement but ample amounts of grace as well. In fact, they see the Old and New Testaments as remarkably consistent in declaring salvation by God's unmerited favor (grace) through faith alone (Eph 2:8–9). In Genesis, we are told that Abraham is credited with a righteousness not his own merely because he believed what God told him (Gen 15:6).

Moreover, in Ps 51 David's plea for forgiveness makes clear that forgiveness and right standing with God is granted apart from perfect obedience:

> Have mercy on me, O God,
> according to your unfailing love;
> according to your great compassion
> blot out my transgressions.
> Wash away all my iniquity
> and cleanse me from my sin.
> (Ps 51:1–2)

Hence, for Evangelicals, God's mercy is given to those who acknowledge their need for it. Yet his patience with the unrepentant doesn't endure forever. We are reminded not to "show contempt for the riches of his kindness, forbearance and patience" and to be mindful "that God's kindness is intended to lead [us] to repentance" (Rom 2:4).

In sum, Evangelicals affirm that judgement and grace inextricably coexist in the Bible. Indeed, grace wouldn't be necessary if judgement wasn't real.

WHAT DO YOU PROPOSE WE REPLACE THE BIBLE WITH?

Critics of Evangelicalism typically reject the Bible's inspiration and authority, but then where do they get their ideas of justice, human dignity and rights, compassion, and so forth? If you were raised in America, Evangelicals say, such ideas unavoidably were drawn from the Bible, the foundational book of Western civilization.

Invariably, when rejecters of Evangelicalism criticize it, they do so on the basis of Christian ideas and principles. Secularism has no well of objective morality from which to draw—no metaphysically rooted standards by which to distinguish good from evil. Secularists are often deluded into thinking that their moral sense emerged from the ether, apart from and without reference to the Bible's moral code.

But the great majority of our cultural mores are traceable to the Bible, even if we have lost sight of their moorings. The Bible's moral instruction is also imprinted on the human heart in the form of conscience, as scripture declares. Hence, the great irony is that opponents of the Bible are forced to steal from its moral teachings in order to judge it.

Evangelicals have often—and continue to—badly fail in living up to Scripture's stringent moral demands. But, how does that impugn the Bible? It's no surprise that Evangelicals hurt others and themselves when they stray from biblical ethics. And when they do, as Tim Keller points out, it is because their Christianity is too weak, not because it is too intense or fanatical.[19]

Fanatically devoted Christians are those that have sacrificed their very lives for the benefit of Christ's enemies—that is what Christ did and what he calls his followers to do as well. Evangelicals get in trouble only when their lives contradict the Bible.

CONCLUSION: STILL FAR MORE DIFFERENT THAN ALIKE

As Evangelicals seek to encounter God in Scripture, there is one overriding fact that they are exhorted to keep foremost in their minds: his transcendence.

The God worshiped by Evangelicals pays followers the huge compliment of dialogue and friendship with him solely on the merit of his own Son, requiring none from believers—only faith. He gives his children laws enabling them to flourish, and yet he is tremendously patient as they—more often than not, laughably—try to keep those laws. The evangelical Christian God engages his people as if they were really like him—with a reasoning mind, a moral sense, and a will to act. In short, he validates the audacious biblical claim that people are made in his image.

But, while Evangelicals can communicate with God due to the attribute of personhood he gifts all people with, the evangelical believer understands that success in approaching God hinges on their awareness that God is still far more different than alike him or her. According to evangelical belief, God meets adherents where they are despite the vast chasm between Him and them. In a word, he condescends, as a loving human father does with his toddler.

Indeed, Evangelicals marvel that they are accepted and pursued by him, especially since he tells them,

> For as the heavens are higher than the earth, so are my ways are higher than your ways and my thoughts higher than your thoughts. (Isa 55:9)

---

19. Keller, *Reason for God*, 56–59.

C

The Upside-Down Kingdom

(Note: Salvation by grace alone through faith alone is an indispensable and foundational pillar of Evangelical Christianity. It was a radical idea in Jesus' time and remains a surprising and counterintuitive idea to this day. One cannot fully comprehend Evangelicalism without apprehending grace, which Jesus often taught about by telling parables, like the one discussed below.)

So the last will be first, and the first will be last.
—MATTHEW 20:16

JESUS TOLD AN OFFENSIVE story about a landowner (representing God) who hires some men to work in his vineyard (Matt 20:1–16). He hires some guys early in the morning and agrees to pay them a day's wage, which at that time equaled one denarius. The landowner goes on to hire more guys at nine o'clock in the morning, noon, three o'clock in the afternoon, and then at five o'clock, and tells them he'll pay them what is right. So far, so good.

But here's the kicker: at the end of the day, the landowner tells his foreman to begin paying the workers, beginning with *the last ones hired*. The guys hired at five o'clock in the evening get a full denarius, so the guys that were hired early in the morning, who've been busting their cabooses for ten hours, naturally expect more than that. But the landowner pays them what was agreed upon and not a shekel more. Needless to say, they grumble and complain, as I know I would.

Hadn't Jesus read the Fair Wage Act of AD 15? The landowner appears to be terribly unjust. His bizarre behavior is not only an affront to our enlightened twenty-first-century sense of fairness and common decency, it was even offensive to the "primitive" folks in AD 30. So we almost expect that Jesus will launch into a stern rebuke of the landowner and tell him in unambiguous terms the unpleasant future awaiting him. But in fact, it's just the reverse: Jesus rebukes the grumbling workers who slaved all day long for that single, measly denarius!

I think this is one of those times where you shake your head and walk away, or you conclude that Jesus really is God. To me, this story is evidence that the gospel isn't a human invention. Any sensible public relations firm in Jerusalem would have strongly advised against the telling of this parable, had Jesus bothered to consult one. And what would the wise men have thought upon hearing such unguarded, reckless, and irrational remarks?

Well, I think they would have gotten it—they were wise men, after all. Unlike me, they would have figured out quickly that this story is about grace, an idea that rankles proud folks like us. Jesus is telling us that God's unmerited favor often comes to the least likely and the most undeserving of people.

You can be galled by that (revealing your spirit of entitlement and self-righteousness) or rejoice in it. I recommend the latter. If you are galled by it, consider the landowner's response to the grumblers who resented getting the same as those who worked far less than they had: "Don't I have the right to do what I want with my own money? Or are you envious because I am generous?" (Matt 20:15).

Jesus is telling us we'll either get exactly what we deserve (so no one can complain of unfairness) or we'll get something that is far better—forgiveness and eternal life—on the basis of Jesus' own perfect record and his cross. Justice is getting what you deserve. Grace is getting what you didn't earn and don't deserve, which bugs people who live by the rules, or at least who think they do.

Consequently, we tend to recoil at the kind of people God saves, which includes crooked government officials, serial killers, drug addicts, adulterers, thieves, fornicators, liars, drunkards, tax cheats, bullies, con men, and so forth. (That God saves such reprobates is curious, but perhaps he is glorified more by loving the truly unlovable than by loving the talented, smart, rich, and beautiful people, as we typically do.)

And good, upstanding folks like you and me? We who have "earned" heaven by virtue of our respectable lives and good works? Funny, we didn't choose our parents, where we grew up, our intellect and educational opportunities, our temperament and personality, our talents, our capacity to work and make money, etc., but we're more than happy to take credit for anything good that our lives may produce. The fact we "good folks" typically credit ourselves for how wonderful we are just shows how lost we are.

You might think that "truly bad" people would be more apt to recognize their moral bankruptcy and seek God's forgiveness. Yet, what makes them "truly bad" is an underdeveloped moral sense, or the inability to recognize their behavior as evil, making it even harder for them to repent and seek God's forgiveness than it is for us "good folks." So it is not a person's degree of "badness" that reveals the need for repentance, although God often uses the consequences of badness to break people's pride and draw them to Christ.

Moreover, the truth is, we good folks are only "good" in comparison to truly bad folks. If we examined ourselves honestly in the light of God's holiness, we'd discover we're truly bad too. So why don't we do so? Because, like the last folks chosen to work in the vineyard, it is by grace alone that anyone—"good" or bad—seeks God's forgiveness through Christ (Eph 2:8–9).

Lastly, and perhaps most importantly, in this parable we find that the last ones hired had been standing out all day waiting for someone to hire them. No one wanted them: these folks are passed over because they don't measure up by the world's standards. They are the emotionally and sexually broken, the physically and cognitively disabled, the socially awkward, the physically unattractive, along with assorted rejects, misfits, outcasts, and losers. Many who are last in the sight of men are first in the upside-down kingdom of Christ.

So, we discover in this parable that God delights to save "the last," purely by grace. As the apostle Paul tells us,

> Brothers and sisters, think of what you were when you were called. Not many of you were wise by human standards; not many were influential; not many were of noble birth. But God chose the foolish things of the world to shame the wise; God chose the weak things of the world to shame the strong. God chose the lowly things of this world and the despised things—and the things that are not—to nullify the things that are, so that no one may boast before him. (1 Cor 1:26–29)

Ponder that if you will.

Part Two

How Evangelical Christians See the World

A

Kindly Stop Stealing from My Worldview

ONE OF THE MORE interesting contradictions in our public debate today is the tendency of fully secular folk to speak of the virtues of love and compassion almost as if they invented them. Political liberals often criticize evangelical Christians because they consider their religious and political beliefs to be woefully lacking in love. The funny thing is that, apart from a loving God, an ethical system based on "love" is as insubstantial as Styrofoam peanuts or pixie dust. To reject God is to reject objective morality completely. Secular liberals are simply stealing from Christianity—and thus breaking the seventh commandment!—when they insist we must love our neighbors and even our enemies.

I'm thinking primarily of secular liberals who reject a God who is a loving and law-giving Father, and who embrace a purely materialistic cosmos. But we might also include religious liberals who acknowledge God's existence but reject the authority and inspiration of Scripture. Such folk are practical atheists since although they affirm God, they doubt his ability to communicate unequivocally with fallen humanity, thus leaving them not much better off than an ardent atheist—stuck in a morass of moral confusion. Often, religious liberals end up ignoring or reinterpreting unpopular Bible passages in accord with what's culturally acceptable.

But for the moment, let's consider the true "atoms are the only things" materialists and their futile attempts to construct some moral framework for living. Think about it: you can't assert that mindless and soulless atoms—which make up everything that we can detect with our senses, including ourselves—are all there is and yet continue to insist that we love our neighbors. Matter doesn't tell us how to live; in fact, matter doesn't speak at all as regards ethical behavior. The transparent atheist is quite right in this regard: morality is purely subjective in a godless universe, existing only as preferences in our minds. Worse, purely material minds are completely unreliable beacons of moral wisdom.

If the cosmos consists merely of atoms ("materialism" or "naturalism"), and life on earth is only the result of a radically improbable string of random events, then moral language has zero validity. To assess one kind of behavior (caring for an orphan, for instance) as superior to a different kind of behavior (beating an orphan, on the other hand) is nonsensical. In the neo-Darwinian view, each behavior was precipitated by molecular reactions in the brain, governed by the laws of chemistry and physics. How can one chemical reaction be morally superior to another?

Hence, how can one blame the orphan-beater for acting in ways controlled by the laws of science, as opposed to someone possessing a rational mind and moral conscience that was gifted supernaturally? Or, why is the one who loves and cares for the orphan deserving of praise, if such love was only the product of a "lucky" series of chemical events in the brain? In short, materialism utterly eviscerates human blame and credit.

Even words like "lucky" are prohibited if atheism is true because they generally are not completely devoid of moral content. Wouldn't it have been just as "lucky" if a cosmos never came into existence and hence life never emerged? To wit, why should the world's existence be better or worse than its nonexistence? If God either doesn't exist or hasn't revealed himself to us, all moral judgements simply reflect our subjective biases and feelings. And, absent God, such judgements would, again, result solely from electrical-chemical events in our brains. Why should we trust them?

Albert Camus, an honest atheist who understood its implications perfectly, concluded that the only serious philosophical problem for the atheist was whether or not to commit suicide.[1] In other words, existence and nonexistence are equally meaningless. In my experience, atheists don't usually embrace this bleak truth—they kid themselves into thinking their bold stand against God is somehow for the good of humankind, thereby conferring an illusory meaning to their existence. Life apparently would be grand if only the theists would repent of their belief and leave us all alone.

CAN LOVE'S UTILITY COMPEL US TO LOVE?

Evolutionary biology offers a glimmer of hope to our atheist and agnostic friends struggling to assert that love has a superior claim than hatred on the human heart. They can point to the emergence of cooperation and kin altruism as crucial evolutionary milestones that resulted in the success of the human species.

But while Darwinists arguably can claim "love"—expressed in cooperation—has had evolutionary utility in advancing the human species, it can never say love is intrinsically good or true. Perhaps love-fueled cooperation helped us become the dominant species on earth by making us more adaptable and less susceptible to nature's tantrums. Consequently, if love has become embedded in our genes over time, then our "love" was programmed into our DNA to increase the odds of individual and group survival. In short, any acts of love we perform are robotic and essentially selfish—solely designed to keep us alive as a species. Not very romantic, huh?

A crafty materialist might argue that since nature has blessed cooperation and altruism, nature itself inherently favors love. But why should that compel us to act accordingly? In a purely material universe, any preference for sophisticated design, intelligence, and

---

1. Camus, *Sisyphus*, 1.

altruistic behavior doesn't exist. These are only subjective value assumptions that we project onto nature. Moreover, our preference for them is merely encoded into our DNA. Materialism doesn't favor complexity over primitivism if the latter is better able to adapt and survive. In short, we have no basis for bragging of our superiority over insects.

Also, to say that nature has a moral character that is "loving" veers right into pantheism. Sorry, but that's a religious idea, my atheist friends. Indeed, Hinduism and some major strands of Buddhism are strongly pantheistic.[2]

Of course, there are psychological benefits to love as well—loving others and being loved by them makes us feel good. But heroin and crack make people feel good too, not to mention contemplating and taking revenge, which "light up" the pleasure centers of the brain.[3] At bottom, materialistic love is merely a DNA-programmed chemical response in our brains, hardly different to how opioids work. For the materialist, there is zero metaphysical grounding assuring us that love is right, good, and true.

Christianity, on the other hand, tells us that love is good and true because the infinite and eternal God of love is also the God of goodness and truth. The three-personal God not only defines and embodies love but models love relationally—something unique among all religions. Jesus, by his life and especially in his death, showed us what real, selfless love is through his own loving obedience to the Father.

Evangelical Christians believe God can only speak truth, and he commands us to likewise love one another. Evangelicals can say, therefore, that love is intrinsically good—it is not merely utilitarian. So, "love your neighbor as yourself" is an objective moral law, binding on all of us. For an atheist, the notion that love is better than hate is a weightless preference or purely biological impulse; it has no transcendent grounding.

---

2. Reese, "Pantheism." See the subsection titled "Pantheism and Panentheism in Non-Western Cultures."

3. Chester and DeWall, "Pleasure of Revenge," 1173.

So next time a materialist argues that our political policies should be loving, gently ask how he or she came to that conclusion, because materialism is no more or less partial to love than it is to hate. "True" love is rooted only in the will and character of the eternal, immutable God.

B

The Imaginary World of John Lennon

(Note: One way to understand the Evangelical worldview is to consider what Evangelicals wholeheartedly reject. There perhaps is no more succinct expression of the ideas in popular culture that Evangelicals find toxic than John Lennon's iconic song, "Imagine," in which the former Beatle casts a utopian vision of a boundary-less world unified under atheism and socialism.)

INTRODUCTION

BACK IN 2011, THERE was a brief kerfuffle when John Lennon's former assistant revealed that at the time Lennon died, the former Beatle was a Reagan supporter and no longer an endorser of radical causes and the leftist peace movement. Fred Seaman assisted Lennon over the last year of his life and observed that Lennon "was a very different person back in 1979 and 80 than he'd been when he wrote 'Imagine.' By 1979 he looked back on that guy and was embarrassed by that guy's naiveté."[1]

Others in Lennon's orbit and in the press quickly pushed back at that, apparently frightened of losing the gifted Lennon as an ideological ally. I get it: everyone wants the cool guy on their side, and Lennon was very cool. Being the smart guy he was, I am persuaded that Lennon figured out that "Imagine" is a sophomorically vapid song and unworthy of an intellect well past its infatuation with hallucinogenics. The Left's reaction to this assertion is a major tell: those confident in their ideological positions aren't threatened by the defection of a fellow traveler who happens to be a pop star.

Clear-eyed fans of Lennon's music should see that the unserious lyrics of "Imagine" are now but a parody of Leftist utopianism. You can't help but chuckle picturing a bunch of misty-eyed Lefties in a group hug, candles aloft, swaying along to the melody, experiencing their kumbaya moment.

In the midst of the Covid pandemic back in 2020, actresses Gal Gadot and Kristen Wiig patched together a series of video clips of themselves and other celebrities singing an "Imagine" verse from their homes, Covid-style, and posted the finished product to YouTube, with the intent of global uplift.[2] Let's just say, it didn't entirely succeed—in fact, there was a backlash against wealthy and materialistic stars glamorizing a world of no possessions. To her credit, Gal Gadot later admitted it was in poor taste.[3]

Nearly a half century has passed since John Lennon's untimely death at age forty in 1980. Yet "Imagine" lives on, capturing the hearts and minds of many. If John Lennon wasn't embarrassed by the song at forty, it seems likely he would have been by now—because the song, despite its continued popularity, presents a shallow and unpersuasive diagnosis of our earthly disharmony, for reasons we'll explore. If you're not familiar with the song or have forgotten the lyrics, the words to "Imagine" are readily available via numerous websites, such as AZlyrics, LyricFind, and Genius. That will

1. *The Week*, "John Lennon."
2. Mench, "Gal Gadot."
3. BBC, "Gal Gadot."

help us avoid a labyrinthine permissions ordeal and keep the lawyers leashed.

IMAGINE WE WERE ALL PERFECTLY VIRTUOUS

The fundamental problem with "Imagine" is the singer's lack of self-knowledge. Poor John looked at how messed up the world is and concluded it was because of things external to him—namely, religion, governments, borders, and property ownership.[4] By the time most folks reach thirty, they typically have discovered what a mess they are deep down inside. Multiply that mess times the eight billion or so other similarly messed up people in the world and what do you have? "One fine mess," as the eminent moral philosopher, Oliver Hardy, would have said.

We live in a broken world filled with broken people. Asking such a sorry group to produce world peace is akin to telling the man in the final agonizing throes of terminal cancer to invent a cure for it.

Jordan Peterson has highlighted how many millennials glom onto big causes—like world peace and, increasingly, climate change—as a means to avoid addressing their own junk.[5] It's a neat bit of deflection: "Hey, I may have a few issues, but that's nothing compared to the earth literally burning up. We need to fix the planet first, then I'll get around to addressing my selfishness, hatred, envy, laziness, lust, gluttony, etc. Because, ultimately, it's not about me! I mean, people are dying!"

Humankind's record over many millennia ought to quash hopes we'll ever live harmoniously, but every generation a new crop of utopians fitted with rose-colored glasses arise to revive faith in "peace on earth" while remaining quite far-sighted as regards their own soul corruption. C. S. Lewis famously observed that loving all of humanity in general is a lot easier than loving the smelly dude next to you on the transit bus.

---

4. Lennon, "Imagine."
5. Peterson et al., *Twelve Rules*, ch. 6.

Lennon's *Imagine* album vividly reveals this contradiction. Along with the title track, "Imagine," it also includes a scathing denunciation of Lennon's former Beatle bandmate Paul McCartney. In the song "How Do You Sleep?," Lennon compares McCartney's recent solo music to the bland, soporific sounds of elevator music, along with other acerbic put-downs.[6] So on the same album, Lennon's affection and lofty hopes for humankind stand alongside his deep animosity for his former musical partner and close friend. Lennon seems oblivious to this contradiction.

It's not that realism about the human condition is entirely missing from the arts.

Bob Dylan and many other musicians, writers, and artists have all bemoaned the pervasive brokenness and absence of harmony in our world,[7] often along with their anguished pleas for world peace.

I wish it were just millennials who assumed this posture. They're young, as was John Lennon when he wrote "Imagine," so they can be forgiven for failing to see that the world's problems originate inside, and not outside, of us. It's very easy to become so focused on the "big picture" and fixing the cosmos that we neglect to cultivate our own gardens, resulting in hurt for those around us.

Let's assume that global warming is truly the man-made catastrophic trend its proponents claim it to be. (We're skeptical it's primarily a man-made problem.) Nonetheless, a global warming firebrand might argue, "How is climate change reducible to the 'mess' inside each person?" First, if we're facing extinction due to global warming, it's because we all enjoy the blessings of a big carbon footprint: houses and cars that consume lots of fossil fuel, along with cell phones, toys, vinyl siding, flat-screen TVs, computers, and a myriad of other oil-based plastic products manufactured at oil-burning factories by companies housed in oil-cooled and oil-heated office buildings.

Moreover, if global warming is truly an existential threat, it behooves climate change activists to immediately embrace a

---

6. Lennon, "How Do You Sleep?"

7. Dylan's song "Everything Is Broken," from the album *Oh Mercy*, is one such example.

carbon-free existence, including ditching the car, abandoning air travel, and forsaking all items manufactured from petroleum, such as plastic, as well as stuff produced in oil dependent plants. But I don't see many of these folks living in huts made of clay with sod roofs. If I expect others to make such sacrifices, shouldn't I be the first to take the leap? Indeed, very few Greenies (I'm looking at you, Al Gore and Leo DiCaprio!) seem willing to do that and yet are more than happy to trumpet coercive big government green "deals," through which they proclaim, "Hey, I'm driving an eighty-thousand-dollar electric car, the least those horrible coal miners can do is to get a new job far from that god-forsaken state of West Virginia."

LOSING OUR RELIGION

"Imagine" dreamers don't get that fixing the world's messes starts with our individual messes. Most religions seem to proceed from this insight, which is why they prioritize personal reflection and repentance over attaining world peace and saving the planet. Lennon's "Imagine" contrarily pines for the day when such annoying religious demands are banished so we can all live in peace, once and for all, free of our supernatural delusions.

Indeed, religion provides a platform for division for human hearts that are hungry for them. But even if we jettisoned religion, there would be no shortage of stuff, as "Imagine" suggests, "worth" fighting over, as the nightly news testifies to us every day: money, power, a potential spouse, the TV remote, a bag of Cheetos, on and on, ad infinitum. Kindly show me a country, past or present, that forbade religion and subsequently experienced an outbreak of love, freedom, and peace. The only social cohesion manifested in countries that squelch religious expression is by virtue of a hot gun barrel.

By the way, Aleksandr Solzhenitsyn, who experienced first-hand the brutal purge of religious belief in the former Soviet Union, observed, "Gradually it was disclosed to me that the line separating good and evil passes not through states, nor between classes, nor between political parties either—but right through every human heart—and through all hearts."[8] That's a pretty on point rejoinder to "Imagine" and a heck of a lot pithier, you may be thinking!

But, back to the idea of dumping God and religion. If I am no longer accountable to God, doesn't that free me up to do what I want to a far greater extent? No lawgiver, no laws, and best of all no eternal consequences to restrain my worst impulses.

NO JUSTICE, NO PEACE

One might protest that there are plenty of consequences for bad behavior already in this world, i.e., "What about prison, fines, and other forms of statutory punishment? There's no need to speculate about folks paying for their crimes in a far-fetched afterlife; we're dishing out the real thing right now on earth!"

The problem is that justice in the home of the free and land of the brave is hit or miss, at best. Many crimes are never solved, "cleared," or "closed," according to the Federal Bureau of Investigation.[9] In other words, the offenders were never identified, apprehended, or prosecuted and thus are presumably free to commit more crimes, unless they're serving time for a separate crime.

The FBI reports that 42 percent of murders and acts of non-negligent manslaughter remain unsolved. (Maybe don't share that with your worst enemies.) Better yet, your odds of getting off scot-free for other infractions are as follows: 59 percent for violent crime, 72 percent for robbery, 73 percent for rape, 85 percent for larceny-theft, and 92 percent for car theft (Porsche dealership, here I come!).[10]

Sentencing in the United States is even more problematic. The median average time served in state prison for murder is just 17.5 years; negligent manslaughter will cost you a paltry 5.3 years;

---

8. Solzhenitsyn, "Notable Quotations." See the section on *The Gulag Archipelago*, part 4, chapter 1, "The Ascent."
9. Statista Research Department, "Crime Clearance Rate."
10. Statista Research Department, "Crime Clearance Rate."

a convicted rapist can expect to spend only 7.2 years in prison; and a miniscule 11 months is the median average of time a convicted car thief gets locked up.[11]

Accordingly, there's less than a one in nine chance I'll be arrested, prosecuted, and jailed for tooling around in that stolen Porsche, and should the odds go against me, I'll likely only spend about a year in the pokey. Those are way better odds than you'll get in Las Vegas or at the racetrack. No wonder crime is so appealing—justice on earth, or at least in the United States, is rarely proportional to the harm incurred, and it is hardly ever restorative for the victims of it.

A popular slogan of the Left is "No Justice, No Peace." Is it reasonable to believe peace on earth is remotely possible as long as 40 percent of murderers and 73 percent of rapists in the United States—a model for justice around the world—are roaming about freely?

Moreover, is earthly peace really conceivable when so many marriages break up and when families themselves are rife with conflict, such that even our kin relationships often resemble the Hatfields and McCoys?

Divine Justice

That's why the fear of God is an important prophylactic against crime. I prefer to live in a society where folks recognize that their bad behavior in the here and now might spoil their eternity. Every word and action on this planet carries far greater weight when there are eternal consequences for them, whereas Lennon's idea that we need only worry about today puts little if any pressure on us to live by the Golden Rule. For many, it's merely a permission slip for hedonism.

Arguably, evangelical Christians enjoy the best of both worlds: while costly and impossible apart from grace, obeying Jesus' command to love others—even our enemies—makes all of our lives better here, with the reward of an infinitely better eternity.

---

11. Kaeble, "Time Served."

Part Two: How Evangelical Christians See the World

Don't Immanentize the Eschaton

Tellingly, "Imagine" represents a sin not only of secular pride but one of religious hubris as well. Evangelicals are not to "immanentize the eschaton"—that is, to attempt to create heaven on earth by radically reinventing the social and political order, apart from God and in advance of Christ's second coming when his eternal throne is established and he fully reigns in the hearts of his redeemed subjects.

By the way, the lovely phrase "immanentize the eschaton" was coined by Eric Voegelin, and popularized by William F. Buckley, among others. You may even have seen "Don't Immanentize the Eschaton" emblazoned on a T-shirt, which would make a wonderful birthday or Christmas gift for someone you love.

At bottom, believing that paradise can be ushered in by human effort alone, as "Imagine" suggests, takes "immanentizing the eschaton"—a fun phrase to repeat—to a whole new level of absurdity.

POSSESSIONS, ANYONE?

Ask most rich Lefties—or even rich Righties, for that matter—if you can take their Ferraris out for a spin, in the spirit of imagining there are no possessions, then try not to choke on the Ferrari's exhaust smoke as it makes tracks.

The idea of sharing everyone else's stuff is pretty cool right up until it's your turn to share. Even when sharing is forced on people by communist governments, it's revealing that the ruling class always gets more and better stuff than everyone else. Even real-life Commies can't transcend their selfish impulses to get and have more than the working class they presumably love and serve.

As best I can recall, John Lennon owned some pretty nice things and engaged in some monumental legal battles to garner his rightful share of the Beatles's massive earnings.

For fans of "Imagine," Lennon was disappointingly bourgeois when it came to royalties and the like, having little interest in sacrificing his fabulous wealth to achieve world peace. Smart man that he was, though, later in life he may even have supported the lower taxes and smaller government policies of Ronald Reagan!

The truth is, "possession-free" societies and nations have had nightmarish human rights' records. Moreover, in order to achieve equality, they end up breaking the causal link between hard work and prosperity, thus impoverishing and even starving their own people, as has been happening in North Korea.

CAN THE WORLD REALLY LIVE AS ONE?

"Imagine" strongly implies that our racial, ethnic, and cultural differences, not to mention our differing views about God, government, economics, and everything else, keep us at each other's throats. If so, then national sovereignty and borders make total sense. Just as parents deal with fighting kids by separating them, national sovereignty and borders are conflict suppressors, reflecting the honest assessment that we just can't get along.

The alternative is to imagine a world in which people have no differences or where conformity is achieved through terror, crushing individuality, and freedom. Perhaps we'll need to wait until we've all taken a quantum leap in handling conflict. Ah, but that just leads us back to fixing what's inside of us—remember, that big ugly disgusting mess? A mess that will require an ocean of Lysol disinfectant before we're ready to abolish armies, nuclear weapons, and national borders? It simply doesn't appear we're much closer to eradicating the ugliness inside each of us than was the average cave man.

At bottom, "Imagine" envisions unity without true diversity, an unappealing state of affairs. The ideal arrangement, but seemingly impossible, is a world that is highly diverse but still unified.

Christians believe that diversity and unity exist in the three-personal Godhead and that believers are called and equipped to mimic the relationship between Father, Son, and Holy Spirit with each other. Without getting into the weeds of Christian doctrine, suffice it to say that, among flesh and blood persons on earth, unity and diversity happens supernaturally or not at all. Christians become unified through the work of the same Spirit, which indwells all believers, without ever losing their individuality (Eph 4:4–6).

The body of Christ across this planet is incredibly diverse, and yet we Christians must confess we have not come close to attaining the unity to which we are called. Still, the closest I've seen unity and diversity coexist on earth has been among Christian believers.

It's therefore okay to be a dreamer in the sense of imagining when the quest for rich diversity and lasting unity both can be fully realized: in heaven. So, I give Lennon props for that, although he likely would prefer if we didn't remind him of that song at all.

C

Why Evangelicals Oppose Multiculturalism

NATURE DESPISES A VACUUM. So do cultures. The marginalization and greatly diminished influence of the Christian worldview in American society doesn't mean that we have no dominant worldview. Christianity has been largely displaced by multiculturalism.

Evangelical Christians see far more in the Bible that just a set of moral rules and a way of escaping the consequences of failing to keep them. Among many other things, Scripture also sets forth a vision for human flourishing in this world that flows from the proper ordering of relationships among and between individuals and the institutions God has established.

Multiculturalists are principally interested in ensuring that the ethos and guiding principles of America are rooted in subjective preferences rather than the objective morality of its Judeo-Christian founding and fairly recent past. Any governmental framework that draws heavily upon the sectarianism of Scripture would naturally be opposed by multiculturalists, even though such a scripturally based worldview actually benefitted everyone, not just Christians.

Part Two: How Evangelical Christians See the World

THE APPEAL OF MULTICULTURALISM

Many—and certainly most all of those inhabiting the culture-forming power centers of academia and the media—believe that multiculturalism is the only viable moral framework for a religiously pluralistic society like America. No religious worldview other than secular humanism, they hold, may be favored in any public sense as being more authoritative and ethically valid than any other. In order to accomplish this, multiculturalists insist that distinctly religious views and arguments are banned from the public debate. Apparently, this is the only way to ensure that there are no religious preferences in public life. In such an environment, Evangelicals largely are compelled to dispense with biblical arguments in order to join the public conversation.

Moreover, multiculturalists typically interpret the Constitution by adopting an extreme interpretation of the First Amendment's protections of religious freedom, wherein they seek to strictly eradicate any religious influences on government. These protections largely were aimed at prohibiting the federal government from interfering with and regulating the religious lives of Americans rather than totally insulating government from religious influence. Multiculturalists seem to forget that the structure of American government, and the inclusion of individual human rights in the Constitution, draws heavily upon Judeo-Christian ideas and biblical theology.

If you want to truly strip government of Christian influence, you'd need to dismantle the Constitution completely, including the separation of powers that serve as checks and balances to prevent a dictatorship arising, not to mention abolish the Constitution's guarantees of individual freedoms and self-governance. These protections from tyranny are rooted in the biblical teachings on man's lust for power, the human tendency to exploit and subjugate those who are weaker or inferior, the God-given dignity that adheres to every single person, and the mandate that humankind worship God in spirit and truth, without interference or compulsion from the state.

C: Why Evangelicals Oppose Multiculturalism

Hence, looking to the particularism of Christianity as the basis for cultural norms is inappropriate for our big-time culture-shapers, despite the fact that America's founding and rise to world prominence are irrefutably tied and indebted to its general adherence to a biblical worldview.

HOW MULTICULTURALISM DELEGITIMIZES FAITH AND WEAKENS CRUCIAL SOCIAL BONDS

While claiming to respect all religions, multiculturalism radically devalues all of them. If all religions are equally true, they must also be equally false. Every religion makes specific (and often contradictory) truth claims, but by virtue of multiculturalism, none of those truth claims can be "truer" than any others. But that's the very essence of truth—it's exclusivity. Thus, if you decide to embrace some religious truth, be prepared to be advised that that truth is only "true for you." It would be inappropriate to expect anyone else to agree with—and even less to abide by—your religiously informed ethics.

It's important to note that multiculturalism isn't merely the province of atheists and agnostics. Religious multiculturalists look at all the nice people of different faiths and conclude they are all deserving of heaven. In their view, we're all climbing that same spiritual mountain, and multiculturalists of faith are generous enough to recognize that these diverse religious paths all lead to the same place. When religious multiculturalists look at God, they are reassured to find that he, she, or it is just like them. Psychologists will recognize this point of view as a textbook case of projection—that is, when folks assume that God is the mirror-image of themselves.

Throughout much of human history, religious truth—not religious relativism—has served as the moral bulwark and cultural glue that is essential to functioning societies. Multiculturalism, atheism, and agnosticism have no record of success in animating and sustaining societies, in shaping the young into virtuous citizens of society, or in generating an agreed-upon ethical grounding that holds people and cultures together. By stripping religious truth of its exclusivity and universality, multiculturalism is left with something as vital, inspiring, and culturally binding as reheated three-day-old oatmeal without the flavorful mix-ins.

When a culture eliminates any transcendent reality as the source of ethics, meaning, and spiritual fulfillment, something else must assume the place of the massive void remaining. In the United States, the weakening of faith in God corresponds to the growing power of the state and its intrusion into virtually every area of American life. To a large degree, both major political parties are guilty of looking to government to solve our most vexing problems.

It is largely by and through the state that multiculturalists seek to elevate and enforce their norms and religious perspective, thereby conferring legitimacy upon multiculturalism as the nation's civic religion. Its claim of religious neutrality belies its disapproval and legal opposition to any religion that encroaches upon public space. With a virtual monopoly over education, government is able to impart the tenets of multiculturalism, both explicitly and implicitly, to American kids. It's no big surprise, then, that belief in the Christian God of truth and attendance at a church adhering to Christian orthodoxy has been rapidly waning in America.[1]

Of course, multiculturalism's religious neutrality comes at the cost of dispossessing all religions of their exclusive, universal truth claims and supplanting these truths with the ethical relativism of multiculturalism. Ironically, at the same time, multiculturalists will often criticize Evangelicals for not adhering to their own beliefs if they put forth policies and positions that multiculturalists disagree with. For instance, if Christians oppose government subsidies for the poor, they can expect to be called "hypocrites" for failing to live up to the Bible's insistence on helping the poor. Multiculturalists don't hesitate to cite Scripture if it advances their objectives, even though they believe Scripture is antiquated and irrelevant.

But lifting multiculturalism to such a preeminent position, buttressed by the power of the state, leaves America in a precarious and untenable position. There's very little evidence from history that various religions (including militant atheism and secularism)

1. Pew Research Center, "Decline of Christianity."

C: Why Evangelicals Oppose Multiculturalism

can coexist with each other in the long term. Oil and vinegar can stay mixed for a little while, but left alone they eventually separate.

In the same way, if the unifying metaphysical grounding of a nation is repudiated by cultural elites and replaced with a competing ethical system opposed by many, that nation will lose cohesiveness, and the chances of ruinous conflict will grow. America is getting a taste of this via our divisive politics, driven largely by the incompatibility of Christianity and multiculturalism.

Multiculturalists often say that the Constitution can be the basis for agreement among Americans around a governing ethos, but their ongoing efforts to reinterpret the Constitution as an infinitely malleable "living document" suggests otherwise. If five Supreme Court justices are able to reinterpret a constitutional provision to suit a particular political faction in a way that the founders never intended, how can the Constitution possibly serve as an anchor of social and political stability?

The Bible, on the other hand, cannot be discarded so easily since it claims to be divinely authored and has served quite well as the foundational text of liberal, Western civilization for centuries. Its critics ought to consider whether American fractiousness and decline is in any way related to the marginalization and declining relevance of the Bible—because it would be foolish, as we argued in the first section, to "bite the book that feeds you."

D

The Biblical Worldview, Sphere Sovereignty, and Evangelicalism's Complicated Relationship with the State

A BIBLICAL WORLDVIEW

WOULD A LOVING, OMNIPOTENT heavenly Father leave us in the dark by being silent, ambiguous, or untrustworthy about the most pressing questions and issues that we humans face? For Evangelicals, the answer is, "Of course not." Evangelicals believe God has mediated his message to humankind through weak and imperfect vessels, and yet his superintendence over every "jot and tittle" of each word in his revelation to humankind, the Bible, ensured its perfection and infallibility in its original form (Matt 5:18).

Evangelical Christians not only regard the Bible as the infallible and authoritative word of God but also as a comprehensive statement embodying all that is necessary for "faith and life." The message of Scripture, moreover, is revealed expressly through its words, yet also through what may be deduced as the "good and necessary consequence" of those words.[1] For instance, the Bible doesn't explicitly expound the doctrine of the Trinity, but the single divine nature of God, subsisting in three persons, is logically evident from the many passages attributing divinity to Father, Son, and Holy Spirit.

Just as a good human father will try his best, albeit imperfectly, to instruct his children on what he knows to be true about how we ought to live, our heavenly Father communicates the same to us through Scripture, except without error (2 Tim 3:16).

A biblical worldview, then, is to adopt the Bible's wisdom on how people and societies prosper, including the proper roles, responsibilities, and authority of the individual, the family, the church, and the state. Evangelicals can—and do—disagree on the implications of biblical principles for public policy. Nonetheless, Evangelicals, in part because they hold to the divine inspiration and authority of Scripture, overwhelmingly agree on the principles themselves. Differences on how biblical imperatives should translate into public policy largely flow from confusion regarding the two distinct roles Christians must traverse in a democratic society.

THE UNIQUE CHALLENGES FACED BY CHRISTIANS IN A DEMOCRACY

If you're a Christian who is against government welfare for the needy, expect some grief from fellow Christians as well as unbelievers. Since Jesus urged his followers to care for "the least of these" (Matt 25:40), when Christians reject government welfare policies, they're denying Christ and being hypocritical, right?

People living in a democracy are both "rulers" and "subjects." They are rulers because they are self-governing, wielding power by voting; but they also are subjects of the rules and policies they

---

1. The Westminster Confession states, in part, "The whole counsel of God concerning all things necessary for his own glory, man's salvation, faith and life, is either expressly set down in Scripture, or by good and necessary consequence may be deduced from Scripture." Westminster Standard, "Confession of Faith," §1.6.

make for themselves. Of course, America is a republic, so we delegate our ruling power by voting for representatives we pay to act on our behalf.

As rulers, individuals presumably make decisions that are in the best interests of the whole nation, not merely in their own narrow self-interest. Yet as subjects, they may pursue their own interests within the limits of the laws they've enacted through their elected representatives. When individuals vote for benefits for themselves but don't vote to collect taxes to pay for them (resulting in public debt) they do a bad job of ruling themselves. They have acted as if they were merely subjects and neglected to govern themselves wisely as rulers.

Further complicating this problem for Evangelicals is that Scripture limits each of the authorities or "spheres" that God has established. He has instituted marriage and family, church, government, and the individual as separate "spheres" and assigned to each different privileges, responsibilities, and limitations. God has also designed them in a complementary fashion so as to maximize human thriving. For instance, married couples are to "be fruitful and multiply," thereby producing and raising virtuous little ones who'll grow up to be productive (and tax paying) members of society. Government, on the other hand, is to maintain order by deterring and punishing evil, which harms individuals, married couples, and families.

The state is not to infringe upon the work and authority of religious entities in providing spiritual nurturance to people, such as expositing the Bible and administering sacraments. Thus, the idea of a state church or any government regulation of the church transgresses the biblical separation of church and state. Americans are fortunate to have a Constitution that largely bars the state from intruding upon the religious beliefs, practices, and expression of individuals and religious organizations.

Individuals, naturally, are not to take the law into their own hands. And while individuals are called to love and forgive their enemies, the state must dutifully prosecute evildoers. If a judge (representing the state), out of personal compassion, "forgives" and sets a convicted murderer free, he has failed to act biblically—he has violated the separation of the individual and state. The biblical idea of distinct roles for individuals, families, the church, and the state is known as "sphere sovereignty" and is a framework articulated and championed by Abraham Kuyper, a nineteenth-century Dutch pastor and theologian.

The "Two Hats" Believers Must Wear in Democratic Societies

Thus, democracy creates a unique predicament for Christians because they find themselves carrying out two distinct roles and wearing two separate "hats." As individuals, they are to imitate the character of God by submitting to his laws—loving God and neighbor, as well as sharing the good news of Christ's redemptive work. This mandate enjoins individuals and is certainly to be pursued by the church collectively.

Separately, as citizens in a self-governing society, Christians are also "little kings," possessing the privilege and power of participating in governance. But for many unbelieving observers and Christians themselves, this is where things get messy and confusing. Should an individual Christian, acting in his or her role as an architect of public policy, help pass laws that dispossess an individual of their home and property for failing to keep up with rent or mortgage payments?

Isn't that siding with heartless financial institutions? Indeed, an individual Christian who owns an apartment building might choose to graciously waive payment or extend time to a tenant whose rent is overdue. But as "ruler," this same Christian must enact and enforce laws that are fair to landowners and banks as well as tenants and borrowers. Individuals, businesses, and entire economies depend upon the fairness of such laws.

Likewise, as noted, a Christian ruler is called to punish and deter evildoers because that in fact is the state's (or "civil magistrate's") biblical calling:

D: The Biblical Worldview, Sphere Sovereignty, and Evangelicalism's

> For the one in authority is God's servant for your good. But if you do wrong, be afraid, for rulers do not bear the sword for no reason. They are God's servants, agents of wrath to bring punishment on the wrongdoer. (Rom 13:4)

Biblically, the state is not the agent of mercy but of justice.

As individuals, evangelical Christians are to deliver grace and truth to gay, lesbian, and transgender persons; but they must also oppose—as representatives of the state—laws that deconstruct and undermine God-ordained and self-evident gender identity. Evangelicals see such laws as flagrantly contrary to Scripture and therefore personally destructive and societally corrosive.

These varying positions rattle the chains of many unbelievers, especially cultural elites, and so they reflexively cry "hypocrisy" and "bigotry" as they vent their disgust at believers.

Of course, when any one of the four spheres—individual, family, church, or state—assumes influence and control not rightfully its own, the impact on the other spheres and society itself will be counterproductive. By far, the greatest usurper of authority from its fellow spheres in America today is the state, which Americans have anointed to play Robin Hood—taking from the rich and giving to the poor—with disastrous results.

As the state radically abrogates those lines of authority, we find ourselves with a massive and intrusive bureaucracy, contributing to widespread family non-formation and break-up, fatherlessness, and the weakening of crucial character-shaping entities like families, churches, and community groups. These sectors of civil society have traditionally insulated individuals and families from the state—but no longer, because the federal government now directly intercedes with misguided financial and other incentives, which sabotage marriage and family stability. In short, societies are healthy when each of the different spheres "stays in its lane," thus maximizing freedom and limiting the size and scope of government.

Ironically, America was founded by people who had good reason to be deeply skeptical of government power. Accordingly, they created a Constitution with *only* express or enumerated powers to limit and check federal power; they undoubtedly would be deeply offended by the size and rapaciousness of our government today, resulting in many Americans becoming heavily reliant upon government largesse. Yet, Americans remain largely quiescent as regards the dangers posed by a leviathan state.

Unless the idea of sphere sovereignty is rediscovered and the God-ordained spheres once again work in a complementary way according to their respective biblical roles, it will be exceedingly difficult to substantially downsize the US federal government and so curtail its growth, intrusiveness, and massive indebtedness in any lasting way.

Bibliography

Augustine. *Confessions.* Translated by Henry Chadwick. Oxford: Oxford University Press, 1991.
BBC. "Gal Gadot Says Imagine Video Was in Poor Taste." Jan. 5, 2022. https://www.bbc.com/news/entertainment-arts-59879071.
Berkowitz, David. "My Testimony." AriseandShine.org. https://www.ariseandshine.org/testimony-translations.html.
Camus, Albert. *The Myth of Sisyphus and Other Essays.* Translated by Justin O'Brien. New York: Vintage, 1991. https://www2.hawaii.edu/~freeman/courses/phil360/16.%20Myth%20of%20Sisyphus.pdf.
Center for Study of Global Christianity. "Frequently Asked Questions." Gordon Conwell Theological Seminary. https://www.gordonconwell.edu/center-for-global-christianity/research/quick-facts/.
———. "Status of Global Christianity, 2024, in the Context of 1900–2050." Gordon-Conwell Theological Seminary. https://www.gordonconwell.edu/wp-content/uploads/sites/13/2024/01/Status-of-Global-Christianity-2024.pdf.
Chalufour, Marc. "What's Behind Boom of Christianity in China." Brink, Feb. 2, 2023. https://www.bu.edu/articles/2023/why-is-christianity-growing-in-china/.
Chester, David S., and C. Nathan DeWall. "The Pleasure of Revenge: Retaliatory Aggression Arises from a Neural Imbalance Toward Reward." *Social Cognitive and Affective Neuroscience* 11 (2016) 1173–82. https://doi.org/10.1093/scan/nsv082.
Clark, Heather. "Survey Shows Many Professing Christians Being Shaped by Culture Rather than Biblical Truth." Christian News, Oct. 8, 2020. https://christiannews.net/2020/10/08/survey-shows-many-professing-christians-being-shaped-by-culture-rather-than-biblical-truth/.
Compelling Truth. "Why Was Slavery Allowed in the New Testament?" https://www.compellingtruth.org/slavery-New-Testament.html.

Bibliography

———. "Why Was Slavery Allowed in the Old Testament?" https://www.compellingtruth.org/slavery-Old-Testament.html.

Copan, Paul. "Servitude in Ancient Israel (Pt. I)." Reasonable Faith, Oct. 15, 2023. https://www.reasonablefaith.org/writings/question-answer/servitude-in-ancient-israel-pt-i.

Got Questions. "Does the Bible Condone Slavery?" https://www.gotquestions.org/Bible-slavery.html.

Holland, Tom. *Dominion: How the Christian Revolution Remade the World*. New York: Hachette, 2019.

James, Sharon. "How Christianity Transformed the World: Biblical Christianity's Impact of the Protection of Life and the Dignity of Women." Sharon James (website), Sept. 4, 2018. https://www.sharonjames.org/article/how-christianity-transformed-the-world-biblical-christianitys-impact-on-the-protection-of-life-and-the-dignity-of-women/.

———. "Tracing Christianity's Impact on Slavery Through the Centuries." Crossway, Oct. 7, 2023. https://www.crossway.org/articles/tracing-christianitys-impact-on-slavery-through-the-centuries/.

Kaeble, Danielle. "Time Served in State Prison, 2018." NCJ 255662. Washington, DC: Bureau of Justice Statistics, Mar. 2021. https://bjs.ojp.gov/document/tssp18.pdf.

Keller, Timothy. *The Reason for God: Belief in an Age of Skepticism*. New York: Riverhead, 2008.

Klett, Leah MarieAnn. "Over Half of US Christians Believe Good Works Will Get Them into Heaven: Study." Christian Post, Aug. 11, 2020. https://www.christianpost.com/news/over-half-of-us-christians-believe-good-works-will-get-them-into-heaven-study.html.

Lennon, John. "How Do You Sleep?" Track 8 on *Imagine*. Apple Records, 1971.

———. "Imagine." Track 1 of *Imagine*. Apple Records, 1971.

Lewis, C. S. *Mere Christianity*. New York: HarperCollins, 2001.

———. *The Problem of Pain*. New York: Macmillan, 2001.

Ligonier Ministries. "What Is the Prosperity Gospel?" July 10, 2023. https://learn.ligonier.org/teachers/ligonier-editorial.

Mauro, J-P. "Report Highlights Increased Levels of Christian Persecution in China." Aleteia, Feb. 23, 2023. https://aleteia.org/2023/02/23/report-highlights-increased-levels-of-christian-persecution-in-china.

McCormick, Micah. "The Obedience and Sinlessness of Christ." Gospel Coalition, Jan. 14, 2020. https://www.thegospelcoalition.org/essay/obedience-sinlessness-christ/.

Mench, Chris. "Gal Gadot Unites the Internet in Anger over Celebrity-Filled Cover of John Lennon's 'Imagine.'" Genius, Mar. 20, 2020. https://genius.com/a/gal-gadot-unites-the-internet-in-anger-over-celebrity-filled-cover-of-john-lennon-s-imagine.

Mohler, Albert. "The God Gene—Bad Science Meets Bad Theology." https://albertmohler.com/2004/10/01/the-god-gene-bad-science-meets-bad-theology/.

Bibliography

Peterson, Jordan, et al. *Twelve Rules for Life*. Toronto: Penguin, 2018.

Pew Research Center. "In U.S., Decline of Christianity Continues at Rapid Pace." Oct. 17, 2019. https://www.pewresearch.org/religion/2019/10/17/in-u-s-decline-of-christianity-continues-at-rapid-pace/.

PursueGOD. "Does the Bible Condone Slavery?" Jan. 23, 2016. https://www.pursuegod.org/bible-condone-slavery-2/.

Reese, William L. "Pantheism." Encyclopedia Britannica, last updated May 23, 2025. https://www.britannica.com/topic/pantheism/God-as-absolute-or-relative.

Reiss, Jana. "Conservative Christians Have a Porn Problem, Studies Show, but Not the One You Think." *Religion News Service*, Aug. 6, 2019. https://religionnews.com/2019/08/06/conservative-christians-have-a-porn-problem-studies-show/.

Solzhenitsyn, Aleksandr. "Notable Quotations." Aleksandr Solzhenitsyn Center. https://www.solzhenitsyncenter.org/notable-quotations.

Statista Research Department. "Crime Clearance Rate in the United States in 2023, by Type of Offense." Statista, Nov. 14, 2024. https://www.statista.com/statistics/194213/crime-clearance-rate-by-type-in-the-us/.

Van Maren, Jonathon. "Atheists in Praise of Christianity?" Stream, May 19, 2020. https://stream.org/atheists-in-praise-of-christianity/.

The Week. "Was John Lennon a Closet Republican?" Last updated Jan. 8, 2015. https://theweek.com/articles/483567/john-lennon-closet-republican.

Westminster Standard. "Westminster Confession of Faith." https://thewestminsterstandard.org/the-westminster-confession/.

www.ingramcontent.com/pod-product-compliance
Lightning Source LLC
Chambersburg PA
CBHW070459090426
42735CB00012B/2620